OZ CLA

GW00359537

250
BEST
WINES
WINE BUYING GUIDE
2012

PAVILION

First published in 2011 by Pavilion Books
An imprint of
Anova Books Company Ltd
10 Southcombe Street
London W14 0RA

www.anovabooks.com

Keep up to date with Oz on his website **www.ozclarke.com**. Here you can find information about his books, wine recommendations, recipes, wine and food matching, event details, competitions, special offers and lots more ...

Editor Maggie Ramsay
Editorial assistant Charlotte Selby
Proofreader Caroline Curtis
Cover & layout design Georgina Hewitt
DTP Jayne Clementson

A CIP catalogue for this book is available from the British Library
ISBN 978-1-862-059207

10 9 8 7 6 5 4 3 2 1
Printed and bound in Italy by L.E.G.O S.p.A Trento

The information and prices contained in this book were correct to the best of our knowledge when we went to press. Although every care has been taken in the preparation of this book, neither the publishers nor the editors can accept any liability for any consequences arising from the use of information contained herein.

Oz Clarke 250 Best Wines is an annual publication. We welcome any suggestions you might have for the next edition.

Acknowledgements
We would like to thank all the retailers, agents and individuals who have helped to source wine labels and bottle photographs.

Prices are subject to change. All prices listed are per 750ml bottle inclusive of VAT, unless otherwise stated. Remember that some retailers only sell by the case – which may be mixed. Please bear in mind that wine is not made in infinite quantities – some of these may well sell out, but the following year's vintage should then become available.

Contents

Introduction

Do we have too much choice? That may seem a strange question for me to ask at the beginning of a wine guide that sets out to give you as wide a range of choices as possible. But I mean it. Would having less choice mean that we found it **easier to make better buying decisions?** Would having less choice remove an onerous layer of stress from our lives? Is the pursuit of choice for choice's sake a false religion that will eventually paralyse us and make us into cannon fodder for the big global brand owners who spend tens of millions of pounds every year persuading us that there is only one choice – theirs?

I began to think that perhaps we do have too much choice when I was reading an article quite unrelated to wine in *The Economist*. There I learned that Tesco offers us 93 varieties of toothpaste. How many of those are genuinely different? How many would actually give us healthier teeth? Tesco can also offer us 91 different shampoos, and 115 different household cleaners. Do I feel better served by this **bewildering choice**? Do I feel empowered – or panic-stricken? Do I settle into the enjoyable challenge of which one will really suit me best, or do I blindly fall back on choosing the one I've seen advertised on the telly?

Choice is a contentious issue. The collapse of Threshers and Wine Rack, then Oddbins, has surely reduced our choice in the High Street. But did these nationally branded shops offer us exhilarating choice? Their disappearance has meant that there are far fewer actual wine shops than there were two years ago, but an **encouraging number of independents** have sprung up – often in the same shop sites – independents who believe that they know what their local audience want and who believe they can supply it. Choice, again. But they will actually be offering us less choice through believing that they know what we want.

A couple of Californian academics came up with some interesting results looking at what motivates us when we're buying jam, chocolate, coffee, lots of things. In the jam test, they set up two sampling tables – one of six jams and one of 24 different jams. Shoppers who stopped to sample the jams got a discount voucher to cash in when they bought one of the jams. There's no doubt more people stopped to sample at the 24 jam table. But when they totted up the results later, 30% of those who sampled from the small six jam collection went on to buy a jar; only 3% of those who sampled from the tempting 24 jam selection bought a jar. **Too much choice had actively demotivated the shoppers,** less choice had encouraged them. Too much choice had created at very least indecision. Does this happen with wine? I'm certain it can, and it often does. Indeed, with wine, indecision might more closely resemble paralysis and panic.

That's why in the old days the commonest advice you got on wine was to pick a wine merchant you liked and trusted and leave it to them to advise you. With the rise of the supermarkets and the High Street chains, this advice became increasingly meaningless. But now, as new independent merchants clamber out from the ashes of High Street collapse, and as more 'speciality' wine merchants become more common – two prime examples are Wine Pantry at London's Borough Market, dealing only in English wines, and Vini Italiani in London's Old Brompton Road, determined to take our knowledge of Italian wine way past just Pinot Grigio and Chianti – perhaps we will increasingly be able to find **a wine merchant to trust** once again.

But it's the supermarkets who dominate our wine world. What about them? The drinks boss of Waitrose said that their research had shown that almost half of consumers find **buying wine** 'difficult', while over three-quarters find it an **'ordeal'**. Which might explain why he also said three-quarters of consumers have a repertoire of just *two* wines. People are genuinely anxious about moving away from what they know they like. Sadly, that is exactly what the Big Brand owners love to hear. Brands exploit consumers' aversion to choice by persuading them there is indeed only one choice.

Now, there should be a big opportunity here for supermarkets. They are the brand in many cases. And some of them are attempting to use this position of consumer loyalty to improve their wine and food offerings. M&S, whose profits jumped 13% this year, say their success is down to offering genuine choice, but not in bewildering amounts. Their wine department doesn't offer a vast spread, but in the last few years has been continually innovative, and sales are up. Waitrose, too, have worked hard on choice being real, **not just an array of me-too labels**, and their profits are up 8%. The Co-op may not immediately sound like the place to shop for wine, but they plan their shops according to what local shoppers want. My local Co-op has more genuine wine choice, especially in the £6.99 to £9.99 range, than some of the Big Boys' megastores that are ten times its size – and the deep-discount promotions are kept clearly separate so that you can see them for the **tomfoolery** that they are.

But could the supermarkets survive without deep discounting? Too right they could, but they don't want to. Half-price deals keep people coming in to your store, and in any case, you make the supplier bear most of the brunt of the cost. 'Marketing support' they call it. 'Financial blackmail' you might call it, if you were a supplier, because if you don't fall in with their demands, you'll find your products thrown out of the store. And yet you're on the horns of a terrible dilemma. Many brands now sell more than 96% of their volume at half price. 96%! Reduce a wine from £10 to £5 and sales can leap 300-fold, from virtually nothing to thousands of cases. And the producer pays. As I look at another bottle of Hardy's Crest – their basic Australian white – **crouching in the corner** of a supermarket shelf at £10.48 **for the statutory period** so that it can then swamp the aisles as a half price 'bargain', **I wonder if any of us are taken in by this any more?** Do any of us really believe it's a £10.48 wine? But we're clearly buying the stuff, or they wouldn't go on doing it. Shouldn't we be buying the supermarket own-label at an everyday low price; shouldn't we be popping into the Co-op or M&S for an interesting range of characterful wines way under a tenner; shouldn't we be asking ourselves, Is wine just a commodity to be bought at the lowest price per unit of alcohol – or does it deserve a bit more attention?

A bit more sympathy would certainly be welcome from the Government. I remember reading the magic words 'no increase' on budget day and for a few optimistic seconds I believed them. Until I realized that the Chancellor had said 'no further increases in duty other than those already in place'. The last Labour budget of 2010 had adopted a plan to increase duty by inflation + 2% until 2015. All George Osborne had to do was **blame the previous government** and count the cash.

Well, I hope he's pleased that we now have the highest duty rate on wine of any country in Europe. With the **15p increase in duty** this year – that was inflation of 5.2% + 2% (and, remember, there's 20% VAT to levy on that duty too) – we're now paying £2.17 in duty + VAT on every bottle of wine. Doesn't it feel good to be paying more wine tax than those famously high-tax anti-alcohol countries Finland and Sweden? Wouldn't it be nice if all those weasel words we used to hear about tax harmonization meant something: Germany, Italy, Portugal, Spain and a host of other EU countries charge no duty at all on wine; France charges all of 3p a bottle. The average price of a bottle of wine in Britain is £4.47; **57% of that is tax**. If you buy a £5 bottle of wine, less than £1 is actually spent on the wine itself from the winery, more than twice that – £2.65 – goes to the government in tax.

Is choice possible at £5 when so little of the cost of the bottle is actually the wine? Amazingly, it still is, just about. And choice is that bit more possible at £7, and at £9 – which is the retail price at which the tax take, £3.30, matches the value of the wine in the bottle. Although, in every country I visit, I hear producers saying that the toxic mix of tax and supermarket greed is making the UK less and less attractive to do business in, there's still some kind of magic about being represented in the British wine world, and producers are still prepared to make a massive effort to play a part in Britain. And it's their wines we need to choose, not the glitzily labelled, slickly marketed, deeply discounted global brands that taste of nothing and of nowhere. That's what this guide attempts to do. **To make choice real again**. To show you where the real wine is, and tell you what price you should pay for it.

Each wine here is among the best in its class. By buying this guide, you've already made the choice – to **drink the best wine** you can this year, at a price you can afford.

Wine finder

Shiraz-Sangiovese, Il Briccone,
Primo Estate, McLaren Vale, South
Australia 26

Sparkling

NV Cienna Rosso, Brown Brothers,
Victoria 119

NV Primo Secco, Primo Estate,
South Australia 118

NV Sparkling Red,Joseph, Primo
Estate, South Australia 121

Sweet

Muscat, Museum Reserve, Yalumba,
Victoria 134

AUSTRIA
White

Dankbarkeit, Josef Lentsch,
Burgenland 50

Grüner Veltliner, 'Mitanaund',
Elisabeth Hausgnost, Wein und
Genuss, Weinviertel 43

Grüner Veltliner, Terraces, Domäne
Wachau, Wachau 57

Riesling, Gaisberg, Birgit Eichinger,
Kamptal 34

Red

Zweigelt, Altenriederer, Wagram 55

Sweet

St. Laurent, Roter Eiswein, Hölzler,
Weinrieder, Niederösterreich 132

CHILE
White

Chardonnay-Viognier-Marsanne-
Roussanne, La Vinilla, Signos de
Origen, Emiliana, Casablanca
Valley 65

P X (M&S), Elqui Valley 73

Sauvignon Blanc, Centauri, O.
Fournier, Leyda Valley 23

Viognier Reserva, Montevista
(Boutinot/M&S), Central Valley 73

Red

Cabernet Sauvignon-Carmenère
(Morrisons), Central Valley 94

Carmenère, Llai Llai, El Bajo de
Totihue, Maipo Valley 80

Carmenère-Shiraz, Los Nucos (Luis
Felipe Edwards/M&S), Rapel Valley
91

Merlot Reserva, Carmen, Casablanca
Valley 44

Pinot Noir, Las Brisas, Viña Leyda,
Leyda Valley 35

Syrah, Touchstone (Viña Falernia),
Limari Valley 29

Rosé

Pinot Noir Rosé, Secano Estate (Viña
Leyda/M&S), Leyda Valley 105

Sweet

Botrytis Semillon, Éclat, Valdivieso,
Curico Valley 135

ENGLAND
White

Bacchus, Chapel Down, Kent 64

Sparkling

English Sparkling Wine, Blanc de
Blancs, Gusbourne, Kent 115

Classic Cuvée, Nyetimber, West
Sussex 114

FRANCE
White

Bordeaux Blanc, Château Bel Air
Perponcher (Vignobles Despagne),
Bordeaux 68

Bourgogne Chardonnay, Vieilles
Vignes, Nicolas Potel, Burgundy
55

Chablis (Brocard/Co-op), Burgundy
61

Chablis, Dom. Vincent Dampt,
Burgundy 32

Chablis, Dom. William Fèvre,
Burgundy 50

Chardonnay, Averys Project
Winemaker, Limoux, Languedoc-
Roussillon 46

Chardonnay, Odyssée, Château
Rives-Blanques, Limoux,
Languedoc-Roussillon 51

Côtes du Rhône Blanc, Domaine de
la Bastide, Rhône Valley 71

Côtes-du-Roussillon Blanc, Palais
des Anciens, Vignerons Catalans,
Languedoc-Roussillon 70

Cuvée Pêcheur, Vin de France 98

Mâcon-Verzé (Corney & Barrow
Selection) Domaines Leflaive,
Burgundy 36

Montagny 1er Cru, Le Vieux
Château, Jean-Marc Boillot,
Burgundy 48

Pouilly Fuissé, 'Vignes Blanches',
Domaine Cordier Père et Fils,
Burgundy 40

Petit Chablis, Domaine d'Elise,
Burgundy 64

Picpoul de Pinet, Coteaux du Languedoc, Domaine des Lauriers, Languedoc-Roussillon 42

Riesling Réserve, Trimbach, Alsace 32

Saint-Véran, En Crèches, Daniel & Martine Barraud, Burgundy 33

Sancerre, Domaine Serge Laporte, Loire Valley 48

Sauvignon Blanc Touraine, Domaine Jacky Marteau, Loire Valley 70

Sauvignon de Touraine, Le Boulay, Dom. Jean-Marie Penet, Loire Valley 67

La Voûte, Vin de Table de France, Terroir Océanique, Chai au Quai 40

Red

Bordeaux, Lea & Sandeman (Carteau-Dabudyk) 76

Bordeaux, Château Gillet (M&S) 90

Bourgogne Rouge, Domaine Gachot-Monot, Burgundy 76

Bourgogne Hautes-Côtes de Nuits (Antonin Rodet), Burgundy 76

Brouilly Cuvée de Tête (Louis Tête/M&S), Beaujolais 53

Cabernet-Merlot, Montgravet, Pays d'Oc, Languedoc-Roussillon 94

Cairanne Côtes du Rhône Villages, 'Les Chabriles', Vieilles Vignes, Domaine Brusset, Rhône Valley 35

Chinon, Cuvée Terroir, Wilfrid Rousse, Loire Valley 74

Corbières, Réserve de la Perrière (Mont Tauch), Languedoc-Roussillon 94

Corbières (Sainsbury's House/Les Vignerons de la Méditerranée), Languedoc-Roussillon 101

Coteaux du Languedoc, Pic Saint-Loup, Domaine Haut-Lirou, Languedoc-Roussillon 77

Côtes du Rhône 'Dame Noire' Mourvèdre, Vignobles Coste, Rhône Valley 37

Côtes du Rhône, Domaine de la Janasse, Rhône Valley 44

Côtes du Rhône, Château Rochecolombe, Rhône Valley 78

Côtes du Rhône (Sainsbury's House/Union des Vignerons des Côtes du Rhône), Rhône Valley 101

Fleurie, La Madone, Vieilles Vignes, Domaine de la Madone/Jean-Marc Depres, Beaujolais 29

Gamay, Fontvel, Côtes du Tarn, South-West France 81

Gigondas, '1806', Domaine du Grapillon d'Or, Rhône Valley 30

Gigondas, Cuvée Tradition, Moulin de la Gardette, Rhône Valley 34

Grenache, Vieilles Vignes, VdP de Mediterranée, Domaine de Cristia, Rhône Valley 79

Minervois, 'Plaisir d'Eulalie', Ch. Ste Eulalie, Languedoc-Roussillon 79

Minervois la Livinière, La Touge Syrah, Château Maris, Languedoc-Roussillon 61

Mourvèdre-Petit Verdot, 'Les Derniers Cépages', Domaine Sainte Rose, Côtes de Thongue, Languedoc-Roussillon 81

Régnié, Domaine Rochette, Beaujolais 75

Réserve de la Saurine (M&S), Vin de France 90

St Chinian, Clos de Bijou, Dom.du Météore, Languedoc-Roussillon 33

Shiraz, Pays d'Oc, Asda Extra Special/Domaines Paul Mas, Languedoc-Roussillon 83

Syrah, Vin de Pays des Collines Rhodaniennes, Jeanne Gaillard, Rhône Valley 47

Visan Côtes du Rhône Villages, Nature, Domaine La Fourmente, Rhône Valley 41

Rosé

Chinon, Cabernet Franc, Goutte de Rosé, Domaine de la Noblaie, Loire Valley 104

Coteaux d'Aix-en-Provence Rosé, La Chapelle, Château Pigoudet, Provence 104

Côtes de Provence Rosé, Château Saint Baillon, Provence 104

Côtes de Provence Rosé, Mirabeau, Provence 105

Grenache Rosé, Vin de Pays des Coteaux de l'Ardèche, Les Vignerons Ardechois, Rhône Valley 107

Grenache Rosé, Plume, Domaine la Colombette, Vin de Pays des Coteaux du Libron, Languedoc-Roussillon 107

Touraine Rosé, Les Cabotines, Domaine Joël Delaunay, Loire Valley 106

Sparkling

2004 Champagne Brut, Premier Cru, De Saint Gall (Union Champagne/ M&S) 114
2004 Champagne Brut, Premier Cru, Pierre Vaudon (Union Champagne) 114
NV Champagne Brut, Blanc de Noirs (Alexandre Bonnet/Waitrose) 117
NV Champagne Brut, Blanc de Noirs, Henri Chauvet 116
NV Champagne Brut, Les Pionniers (P & C Heidsieck/Co-op) 118
NV Champagne Brut, Premier Cru (Union Champagne/Tesco Finest) 116
NV The Society's Champagne Brut, Private Cuvée (Alfred Gratien) 115
NV Champagne de Bruyne, Cuvée Absolue Brut Rosé 116
NV Crémant de Bourgogne, Blason de Bourgogne Rosé, Burgundy 118

Sweet

Chaume, Château Soucherie, Loire Valley 132
Rivesaltes Hors d'Age, Reflexió, Castell Pesillà, Languedoc-Roussillon 133

GERMANY
White

Riesling Kabinett, Ürziger Würzgarten, Dr Loosen, Mosel 58
Riesling Kabinett, Piesporter Goldtröpfchen, Hain, Mosel 60

HUNGARY
White

Chenin Blanc-Pinot Grigio-Királyleányka, Eva's Vineyard, Hilltop Neszmély, Észak-Dunántul Region 99
Furmint, Royal Tokaji 28
Pinot Grigio, Mátra Mountain 87

ITALY
White

Arneis Roero, Marco Porello, Piedmont 48
Cortese Piemonte (Araldica/M&S), Piedmont 86
Falanghina Beneventano (La Guardiense co-op/M&S), Campania 86
Fiano-Falanghina-Greco, Triade, Campania 66
Gavi (Fratelli Martini Secondo Luigi/Tesco Finest), Piedmont 69
Gavi di Gavi, Fratelli Levis, Piedmont 43
Gewürztraminer, Castel Turmhof, Tiefenbrunner, Alto Adige 52
Greco di Tufo, Vesevo, Campania 27
Pecorino, Sistina, Terre di Chieti, Citra, Abruzzo 67
Pinot Grigio, Villa Malizia, Venezie 99
Soave, Passo Avanti, Cantina di Monteforte, Veneto 70
Soave, Vignale, Veneto 89
Soave Classico (Equipe/Tesco), Veneto 99

Verdicchio dei Castelli di Jesi Classico (Piersanti/Sainsbury's TTD), Marche 88
Verdicchio dei Castelli di Jesi Classico, Moncaro, Marche 89
Verdicchio dei Castelli di Jesi Classico Superiore, Pievalta /Barone Pizzini, Marche 66
Vermentino della Maremma Toscana, Pagliatura, Fattoria di Magliano, Tuscany 25
Vernaccia di San Gimignano, Tenuta Le Calcinaie, Simone Santini, Tuscany 51

Red

Bardolino, Recchia, Veneto 90
Negroamaro Salento, Tenute al Sole, Cantine Due Palme, Puglia 92
Negroamaro, Terre di Sava, Puglia 91
Puglia Rosso, Anarkos, Racemi, Puglia 79
Primitivo, Polvanera 14, Gioia del Colle, Puglia 75
Primitivo del Tarantino, I Monili, Racemi, Puglia 82
Rosso Piceno, Moncaro, Marche 95
Rosso Toscana, Le Cupole, Tenuta di Trinoro, Tuscany 52
Sangiovese di Romagna (Schenk Italia/M&S), Italy 91
Santa Cecilia, Planeta, Sicily 49
Sherazade, Donnafugata, Sicily 74
Valpolicella Ripasso (Casa Girelli/ Co-op), Veneto 82

Rosé
Nero d'Avola Rosé (Cantine Settesoli/Tesco Finest), Sicily 106
Sparkling
NV Asti Dolce (Araldica/Sainsbury's), Piedmont 121
Moscato d'Asti, Sourgal, Elio Perrone, Piedmont 120
NV Prosecco Brut, San Leo 120
Sweet
Brachetto d'Acqui, Cavallino, Il Cascinone, Piedmont 135
Vin Santo del Chianti Rufina, Villa di Monte (Fattoria di Vetrice/M&S), Tuscany 133

NEW ZEALAND
White
Chardonnay, Cowrie Bay, Gisborne 86
Chardonnay Heretaunga, Lone Range (Capricorn Wine Estates/M&S), Hawkes Bay 45
Pinot Gris, Lismore, Ata Rangi, Martinborough 25
Riesling, Main Divide, Pegasus Bay, Waipara 58
Sauvignon Blanc, Freeman's Bay, Winemaker's Reserve, Marlborough 88
Sauvignon Blanc, The Ned, Marisco Vineyards, Marlborough 36
Sauvignon Blanc, Ngakuta Bay, Marlborough 87
Sauvignon Blanc, Tiki Ridge, Marlborough 67
Sauvignon Blanc, Urlar, Gladstone 51

Sauvignon Blanc, Zephyr (Glover Family Vineyards/M&S), Marlborough 53
Red
Pinot Noir, Asda Extra Special/Wither Hills, Marlborough 75
Pinot Noir, Domain Road Vineyard, Central Otago 59
Pinot Noir, Waipara West, Waipara 24
Syrah, Man O'War, Waiheke Island 21
Rosé
Sauvignon Blanc Rosé, Southbank Estate, Marlborough 105
Sparkling
NV Pelorus, Cloudy Bay, Marlborough 117
NV Sparkling Sauvignon Blanc, Lindauer 119
Sweet
Late Harvest Chardonnay, Waipara West, Waipara 134

PORTUGAL
White
Vinho Verde, Quinta de Azevedo, Sogrape 72
Red
Ciconia, Touriga Nacional-Syrah-Aragonez, Herdade de São Miguel, Alentejano 80
Dão, Flor de Nelas Seleção 80
Douro Red, Crasto, Quinta do Crasto 57
Touriga Nacional, Alentejano (Falua Sociedade de Vinhos/Tesco Finest) 82

Fortified
2005 Late Bottled Vintage Port (unfiltered, bottled 2010), Fonseca 129
1994 Vintage Port (Symington Family Estates/Tesco Finest), Portugal 128
10-year old Tawny Port, Taylor's 128
Crusted Port, Graham's 129
Pink Port, M&S 129
Full Rich Madeira, Henriques & Henriques 127

ROMANIA
White
Viognier-Tamaioasa Romanesca, Scurta Vineyard (Cramele Halewood), Dealurile Munteniei 72

SOUTH AFRICA
White
Chenin Blanc, Fairview, Darling 68
Sauvignon Blanc, Cambalala, Western Cape 100
Sauvignon Blanc, Crow's Fountain (Villiera Wines/M&S), Stellenbosch 38
Sauvignon Blanc, Spice Route, Darling 45
Red
Cabernet Franc, Raats, Stellenbosch 54
Pinotage, Delheim, Simonsberg-Stellenbosch 56
Shiraz, Dolphin Bay, Western Cape (M&S) 95

Shiraz-Viognier, Douglas Green, Western Cape 93
R M Nicholson, Rustenberg, Stellenbosch 31
Rosé
Pinotage Rosé, La Capra, Fairview, Paarl 106
Sweet
La Beryl Blanc, Fairview, Paarl 133

SPAIN
White
Airén-Sauvignon Blanc, Gran López, La Mancha 89
Albariño, Viña Taboexa (Bodegas La Val), Rías Baixas, Galicia 65
Albariño, Orballo (Bodegas La Val/M&S), Rías Baixas 46
Albariño, Rías Baixas, Eidos de Padriñán, Adega dos Eidos, Galicia 22
Albillo, Picarana, Bodega Marañones, Vinos de Madrid 34
Macabeo Blanco, Las Corazas, Vino de la Tierra de Castilla 98
Rioja Blanco, Valdepomares (M&S) 87
Rioja Blanco, Bodegas Muga 24
Rueda, Orden Tercera, Javier Sanz, Castilla y León 69
Rueda, Verdejo, Palacio de Bornos, Castilla y León 69
Rueda, Verdejo, Quintaluna, Ossian, Castilla y León 71
Red
Clos Lojen, Bodegas y Viñedos Ponce, Manchuela 37

Garnacha, Calatayud, Cruz de Piedra (Bodega Virgen de la Sierra co-op) 93
Montsant, Planella, Joan d'Anguera, Catalunya 39
Priorat, Humilitat, Christophe Brunet & Franck Massard, Vinoamory Fantasia, Catalunya 59
Ribera del Douro, Spiga, O. Fournier 20
Ribera del Duero Crianza, Viña Pedrosa, Bodegas Pérez Pascuas, Castilla y León 42
Rioja, Marques del Norte (Asda) 101
Rioja Reserva Especial, Viña Ardanza, La Rioja Alta 21
Shiraz, La Tinta, Bodegas López Mercier 102
Tempranillo, Sabina, Navarra 93
Tempranillo, Toro Loco, Utiel Requena 102
Tinta de Toro Joven, Balcon de la Villa (Bodega Covitoro/M&S), Toro, Castilla y León 83
Viña Decana Reserva, Utiel-Requena 95
Vino de la Tierra de Extremadura (M&S) 92
Rosé
Viña Sol Rosé, Torres, Catalunya 107
Sparkling
Vintage Cava, Chardonnay, Blanc de Blancs, Single Estate, San Cugat (Freixenet/M&S) 119

Sweet
Moscatel Oro, Floralis, Torres 136
Moscatel de Valencia, Cherubino Valsangiacomo/Tesco) 136
Fortified
Amontillado Maribel, Sánchez Romate 125
Dry Amontillado Sherry, Aged 12 years, Emilio Lustau/Sainsbury's TTD 124
The Society's Fino, Sánchez Romate 126
Manzanilla San León, Bodegas Argüeso 124
Manzanilla, Special Reserve (Bodegas Barbadillo/Tesco Finest) 127
Manzanilla (Bodegas Williams & Humbert/M&S) 126
Dry Old Palo Cortado, Emilio Lustau/M&S 125
Dry Oloroso Sherry, Aged 12 years, Emilio Lustau/Sainsbury's TTD 124
Dry Old Oloroso, Emilio Lustau/M&S 126

USA
White
Viognier, Breaux Vineyards, Virginia 56
Red
Zinfandel, McManis Family Vineyards, California 44
Old Vine Zinfandel, Van Ruiten, Lodi, California 60

Index by producer/ brand

TOP
250

TOP 100

The newspapers this year have been full of stories about the insane prices being charged for the top wines from places like Bordeaux. If you're wondering, Is that relevant to me? Will I ever afford to drink top wine again? – the answer is, No, it isn't relevant, and yes, you can drink wines with fabulous flavours for less than £20, less than £15, less than £10. I judge my Top 100 wines on the flavours I like best, not on the price, not on the glitziness of the label. 20 of my Top 100 are less than £10 a bottle. Half of my Top 100 are between £10 and £15. Of course, if you're looking for the smartest red Bordeaux or Burgundy, the top Barolo, the leading California cult Cabernet, you won't find them here, because you pay as much for the prestige as for the actual wine. But if you care about flavours – thrilling flavours, challenging flavours, unusual, unbeatable, irresistible flavours, often from grape varieties or from regions you're not familiar with – that's what you'll find here. Sprinkle a few affordable classics – and that's my Top 100 for 2012.

This chapter lists my favourite wines of the year, both red and white:
▮ = red wine ♀ = white wine

1   2004 Riesling Wigan, Peter Lehmann, Eden Valley, South Australia, 12.5% abv
♀ Great Western Wine, £12.85, Vin du Van, £15.75

It's almost impossible to describe to people how Riesling can transform from a sharp, zesty, lean-boned youngster into a wine that is rich and buttery, mellow and warm – and yet is still bone dry. But then, hardly anyone offers us the chance to enjoy mature Riesling. This wine is simply thrilling stuff. All you anti-Rieslingites, step up. You to taste this. How can I describe something as mellow yet petrolly? How can the sharp squirt of lime zest oil fold into the Sunday morning contentment of fresh white toast with the butter melting into the bread? Surely the wine will be soft – and glimpses of coffee-chocolate cream and custard say, yes, it's soft and plush – but it isn't. That wonderful vibrant lime peel citrus scent is always there, laughing and teasing every time the custard and cream try to cuddle and cajole your palate into thinking this is easy peasy stuff. It isn't. These flavours are a challenge, a paradox; a paradox of genius. I've tasted the 2005: it's just as good.

2   2005 Ribera del Douro, Spiga, O. Fournier, Castilla y León, Spain, 14.5% abv
♟ Butlers Wine Cellar, D Byrne, Martinez Fine Wine, Penistone Court Wine Cellars, c.£24

Brilliant stuff. There are more famous Ribera del Douros than this. There are more expensive ones by far – but I challenge any of them to offer a more sumptuous, thrilling experience than this. It's massively dark and serious, it's bulging with dark fruit verging on the overripe, but the beauty of the wine is that it treads a

hedonist's tightrope between utterly rich black fruit and a shimmering, mouthwatering freshness. The fruit is lush blackberry and black cherry with a teasing hint of prunes, almost syrupy rich, but with the tingly acidity of damson skins and a firm but reassuring tannin making it into a triumphant mouthful.

3 2008 Syrah, Man O'War, Waiheke Island, New Zealand, 14% abv
🍷 Harvey Nichols, £18, Noel Young, £17.15

I'd never tasted this wine until last year, when I visited Man O'War, a wild, isolated patch of Waiheke Island, way out in the bay opposite Auckland. From dozens of dizzying little plots angled this way and that, swept by the salty ocean wind yet stroked by a warm southern sun, comes this remarkable wine. There's no other vineyard quite like Man O'War, and there's no other Syrah like this, rich and scented, dry, yet packed with loganberry and blackberry fruit awash with the creaminess of white chocolate – and somehow all this lush flavour is pushed aside by a brush of grilled lamb chop fat and the crunchy green tastes of celery and peppercorn sprinkled with coriander seed.

4 2001 Rioja Reserva Especial, Viña Ardanza, La Rioja Alta, Spain, 13.5% abv
🍷 armit, £24.99, Noel Young, £24.49

It's very rare that you can taste a wine and look right back into the mists of your wine life and say, this hasn't changed. I still remember tasting – well, drinking – Viña Ardanza at university, at a time when most reds were acidic and bitter and you had to down them holding your nose, and thinking, how can a red wine taste so lush, so gentle and approachable and yet so serious and satisfying? That's still the way it is. Vanilla and coconut – they were always there. It's the coconut of coconut fudge with the stringy bits to chew on –

mixed with pale strawberry and old red cherries and a savoury quality that made me think of Shippam's meat paste. If that sounds old-fashioned, well, it is. Some of the best Rioja is decidedly old-fashioned. And this is some of the best Rioja. Ardanza have made only three Reserva Especials. In 1964, in 1973 – and now this one, from 2001.

5 **2010 Colombard, La Biondina, Primo Estate, Adelaide, South Australia, 12% abv**
♀ AustralianWineCentre.co.uk, £9.99

This is one of Australia's most remarkable white wines. Born in the unheralded dusty plains north of Adelaide from a patch of the decidedly untrendy Colombard grapes, it seems to change and get better with every vintage and throws up an endless array of unlikely flavour combinations. This year it somehow mixes the passionfruit's thrillingly sharp yet scented personality with the crispness of a green apple and the crunchiness of cos lettuce. But it's not finished. The texture is as clean as the glistening blade of a rapier, yet there's some savoury warmth like polished leather and a nip of persimmon bitterness. Where did all that come from? It'll be different next vintage.

6 **2009 Albariño, Rías Baixas, Eidos de Padriñán, Adega dos Eidos, Galicia, Spain, 13% abv**
♀ Lea & Sandeman, £13.95

Albariño is reckoned to be the best of Spain's fresh, scented, white grapes, and is most successful when grown in Rías Baixas in the damp, windy, far north-west of the country. These wines carry the mark of pale summer sun regularly washed away by the splash of Atlantic brine and the driving wind from the West. It all makes for great flavours – the fruit is medlars and hard-skinned northern apples, there is some floral scent, though it's whipped away on the gale, and the fresh acidity is drenched in sea salt and the moist minerals of the rock pool.

7   2008 Shiraz Blue Chip, Eldredge, Clare Valley, South Australia, 14.7% abv

℗ AustralianWineCentre.co.uk, £14.99

This is how the great Barossa Shirazes used to taste before fashion and the crazed eyes of wine critics turned their fickle attention on the wine style and persuaded the growers to make ever bigger, ever more alcoholic, ever less drinkable styles. This is something of a powerhouse, granted, but the fruit is sweet and focused and a delight to the tongue. It oozes purple plum flavours, bulging with ripeness, but scented with warm autumn orchard air and streaked with blackcurrant juice. Season that with licorice, menthol and a spoonful of your favourite cough medicine – and you've got a picture of Barossa Shiraz as it used to be.

8   2009 Sauvignon Blanc, Centauri, O. Fournier, Leyda Valley, Chile, 14% abv

℗ D Byrne, Noel Young, c.£14

People don't think that Sauvignon wines should be aged even when they come from France's grandest vineyards, so when the grapes are grown on some of the newest acres in Chile, surely you wouldn't be aging the wine? But that's exactly what Iberian whizzkid José Manuel Ortega – scourge of complacency in Spain, Argentina and Chile – sets out to do. He takes wonderful, tangy, fog-cooled Leyda fruit and makes it into a deep, complex, mouthfilling wine of limitless possibilities. There's plenty of crisp fruit – green capsicum, coffee beans, gooseberries and apple peel are all churning around in there – but it's not sharp-edged, and the texture is, if anything, slightly syrupy, with the softness of a little oak and the savouriness of freshly toasted cashew nuts.

9 2010 Rioja Blanco (barrel-fermented),
Bodegas Muga, Spain, 13% abv

♀ Majestic, £10.99

Retailers find it so easy to sell red Rioja, but say they
have a devil of a time trying to sell the white. Well, it's a
pity, because white Rioja can be world-class stuff, yet,
because none of you will buy it, the price stays temptingly
low. This is still very young, but it will age for donkey's
years. Already it's spicy and exotic, ripe white peach and apple flesh darted about with clove and cinnamon
and juicy acidity, and just beginning to reveal its future. Over five to ten years it'll develop a most wonderful
flavour of golden cling peaches, custard and savoury cream. One of Europe's most undervalued whites.

10 2009 Pinot Noir, Waipara West, Waipara, New Zealand, 14% abv

♟ Waterloo Wine Company, £16

Waipara West is a splendid, isolated winery way off the beaten track in New Zealand's South Island. It
makes famously haughty whites, but this Pinot is altogether more companionable, offering a lovely mix of
weight and freshness and the scent of herbs. There's a little toasty oak, but not enough to disturb the sweet
beauty of ripe raspberries and red cherries, and the herb scent has no bitterness, just an ethereal fragrance
drifting through the wine.

11 2010 Pinot Gris, Tim Adams, Clare Valley, South Australia, 13% abv

♀ AustralianWineCentre.co.uk, Tesco, £11

The great Tim Adams is gradually spreading his wings, both with new vineyards and with new grape
varieties. He's never been a Chardonnay fan, so thought he'd give Pinot Gris a go – not in the light, quaffing

Pinot Grigio style, but in something more closely modelled on the superb Pinot Gris of Alsace in northern France. This has a slightly copper cast – which is a delight to see. Pinot Gris is a pink grape and if you try to remove its colour, you remove flesh and texture too. The utterly beguiling honeysuckle scent runs right through the wine, gaily mixing with the crispness of Cox's apples and lemon zest and the savouriness of tobacco. It's gorgeous now. If you age it, the wine will develop unctuous quince and apricot depth.

12 2010 Pinot Gris, Lismore, Ata Rangi, Martinborough, New Zealand, 14.5% abv
♀ Fortnum & Mason, Liberty Wines, The Sampler, £21.99

Ata Rangi are uncompromising winemakers, and while much of New Zealand has become wedded to producing light, simple Pinot Grigio styles, Ata Rangi have established their Pinot Gris vines using ancient 19th-century sources – famous for glorious flavours and tiny crops. Great Pinot Grigio can have a slightly unwashed character, and so it is here; this is lush, waxy wine flowing with honey and goldengage syrup but also a more burnished fruit – bronze-skinned pears, a fig and almond treacle tart. It all seems so honey-dewed, honey-dripped, honey-drizzled, until you realize there's something scuffing your tongue, something dusty, heat haze, the peach skin you chew, then do you spit or swallow? Swallow – then drink deep once more.

13 2010 Vermentino della Maremma Toscana, Pagliatura, Fattoria di Magliano, Tuscany, Italy, 12.5% abv
♀ Lea & Sandeman, £14.75

Even in the red wine heartland of Tuscany, Italy's white wine revolution continues to roar ahead. Maremma is a pretty warm coastal area of Tuscany, but the Vermentino grape is well adapted to Mediterranean conditions. As with many of the best new wave Italian whites, it suggests various flavours rather than offering them like great wodges of this

and that all piled on a plate. This treads the line between the gently crunchy fruit of apple peel and not-quite-ripe peaches, aided by a whiff of lime and apple blossom floral scent, and then seems to promise something more exotic and lush, led by honey and autumn orchard sweetness. But it's just a promise; the beauty of the wine is that you're satisfied with the promise – perhaps the fulfilment would have been a touch too much.

14   **2008 The Cigar, Yalumba, Coonawarra, South Australia, 14% abv**
🍷 Flagship Wines, S H Jones, Noel Young, £15–16

Yalumba has done a better job of preserving tradition while embracing progress than almost any other Aussie winery. This has the hint of pinging, self-confident purity of dark fruit that made Coonawarra famous generations ago, and which has been in short supply more recently. The fruit is dark yet juicy, a delicious syrup of blackcurrant, black plums and a judicious swirl of Fowler's Black Treacle. And the scent? Well, it's piercing, it's heady, and it's minty. Spearmint, chewing gum, mint toffee, mint creams – toothpaste? Well, perhaps not, but make up your own mind.

15   **2009 Shiraz-Sangiovese, Il Briccone, Primo Estate, McLaren Vale, South Australia, 14.5% abv**
🍷 AustralianWineCentre.co.uk, £12.50

Joe Grilli is one of very few people to match Sangiovese with Shiraz – but it makes absolute sense. In McLaren Vale, the Shiraz can get just a bit too ripe and chunky, but the Sangiovese holds on to its acidity and grippy herb scent as though its life depends on it. The Shiraz dominates, with its lush, ripe blackcurrants, its chocolate and its Jersey cream gooiness, but the Sangiovese throws in a leaner streak of dry, chewy fruit, savoury scent and menthol bite that makes for a great, original drink.

16 2009 Greco di Tufo, Vesevo, Campania, Italy, 12.5% abv
♀ Harvey Nichols, Liberty Wines, Noel Young, £13.99

A wonderfully original white from the Italian hills, from the area of Campania, surrounding Naples. The potential of these vineyards has long been recognized, but until recently there were very few wineries capable of transforming this famously volcanic landscape and its ancient vineyards into anything vaguely attractive. That's all changed; this is magical stuff – with loads of juicy fruit led by pears and bananas, creamy in texture, scented with almond flowers and pear blossom, anise and spearmint leaf, yet in the far distance you can just sense the smoky growl of the lava flow.

17 2009 Sangiovese-Shiraz, Coriole Vineyards, McLaren Vale, South Australia, 14.5% abv
🍷 S H Jones, c. £11

Shiraz-Sangiovese is rare enough in Australia, but Coriole go one further and make a wine that is mostly Sangiovese with just a helping hand from the rich juiciness of Shiraz. The wine is still rich, but nowhere near as lush and hefty as many McLaren Vale reds are. There is blackberry fruit, but it's mashed together with red cherry and sun-ripe tomato, and there's some scent – a brief flowering of blossom that quickly gives way to the sterner aromas of hillside herbs. Chewy tannin and bright acidity make your mouth water in a most un-Australian way, and then right at the end, almost apologetically, lushness returns with rich loganberry syrup and the warm whiff of fresh roasted cashew nuts.

18 2008 Furmint, Royal Tokaji, Hungary, 14% abv
♀ Laithwaites, Majestic, £9.99

Furmint is an important Hungarian grape variety, but since it's almost always made into rich Tokaji wine, it's a bit difficult to know exactly how it's supposed to taste in its unadorned state, without the support of sweetness. Well, strange might describe it; wild, maybe; unexpected, certainly. So if you're ready for that, let's go. High acidity is the first thing – not searing, scything perhaps. But you need the acid because this wine is awash with the lushness of beeswax and syrup and the unlikely companions of pineapple and quince jelly. It's rich, not really totally dry, and a welcome reminder of the great, fiery whites of Hungary generations ago.

19 2010 Riesling, Tim Adams, Clare Valley, South Australia, 11.5% abv
♀ AustralianWineCentre.co.uk, Tesco, £10.29

Tim Adams Riesling has been one of my favourite Aussie whites for years now. When it's young it usually has a citrus tang and mineral power that can be slightly unnerving, but which you quickly grow to love. This does have a delightful lime flower and cedar scent and the flashing acidity of lime zest, but it is a little softer than usual, with mild apple flesh and even, good gracious, a suggestion of Danish pastry softness. Whatever

next? But it does mean that if you're not accustomed to the bright-eyed attack of a young Adams Riesling, perhaps you'll actually prefer the softer style.

20 2009 Fleurie, La Madone, Vieilles Vignes, Domaine de la Madone/Jean-Marc Depres, Beaujolais, France, 14% abv
🍷 Domaine Direct, £15.30

The wonderful Beaujolais wines of the 2009 vintage were thrilling and irresistible as soon as the grapes piled into the vat. From top properties like this, the flavours were almost overpowering in that first flush of youth, crazy adolescents needing to shed some energy and calm down a bit. Now, they're still almost ridiculously ripe and tasty, but there's just a hint of mellowness entering in. This is fabulously scented with lilies – the flowers and the stems – and a haze of mineral dust. In your mouth the perfume stays, but there's an explosion of rich strawberry, even a hint of raisin ripeness and the appetizing furry rub of pumice stone.

21 2009 Syrah, Touchstone (Viña Falernia), Limarí Valley, Chile, 14.5% abv
🍷 Vintage Roots, £7.95

This is one of the great cool-climate Syrahs of the New World, yet the vineyard is the nearest thing you can get to the broiling Atacama Desert without requiring artificial respiration. Chile is full of paradoxes like this. All the more reason to recognize that this long, thin sliver of a country on the far side of the Andes is rapidly proving itself to be a place of almost unlimited variety. Anyway, forget about the desert, just revel in the flavour – and the price. World-class wine at £7.95. The scent of this is heady yet restrained: peppertree flowers, sandalwood, balsam sprinkled with mountain minerals, and yet the flavour is intense blackberry and ripe black plum – and the texture is truly dry, any self-indulgent plushness sucked out of it by the desert sun.

22 2008 Gigondas, '1806', Domaine du Grapillon d'Or, Rhône Valley, France, 14.5% abv

🍷 James Nicholson, Stevens Garnier, £15.49

Gigondas is a village right next to Châteauneuf-du-Pape in the southern Rhône Valley, where the vineyards positively broil. This can mean the wines are just too thick and jammy to be a lot of fun. But there are an increasing number of good growers in Gigondas who know how to handle these conditions, and – especially in years like 2008, when it isn't quite so hot – wonderfully heady yet balanced wines can appear. This is certainly rich, but it stays appetizing, its flavour dominated by the rocks and herbs of the surrounding hills, not by sun-baked fruit. The fruit's there, a lush mix of loganberry and blackberry and a spoonful of dark syrup, but above all it's the warm, wild scent that grabs me – rosemary, thyme and bay, and warm rocks that might have been splashed with fragrant bath oil.

23 2009 Malbec, Achaval Ferrer, Mendoza, Argentina, 14.5% abv
🍷 Corney & Barrow, £14.59

Unfiltered, unfined, unmucked about with – this is supposed to be Malbec in all its naked glory as God intended. Well, if Malbec is supposed to be a genial giant of a grape, then here's the real thing. The smell makes you wonder whether the grapes baked on the vine, but one mouthful tells you they were impressively ripe, but not overdone. The wine is dense, smooth, broad; tannic, yes, but in a manner necessary to calm down the rich raspberry syrup and chewy damson fruit, the leather and clean fish oil texture and the plum-skin acidity that even carries a tiny trail of floral scent in its wake.

24 **2009 Shiraz, The Lodge Hill, Jim Barry, Clare Valley, South Australia, 14.5% abv**
The Co-operative Group, £9.99, Flagship Wines, £11.25

Clock that price, then listen to these flavours. Licorice, Harrogate toffee, prunes, blackcurrant, mint chocolate creams, and even a handful of earth and some plum-skin chewy acidity. Everything you could want in a Shiraz. It's not the most dense Shiraz you'll find – it comes from the highest, coolest vineyard in the Clare Valley – but who wants dense all the time? It's a rollicking good glass of Aussie grog.

25 **2009 R M Nicholson, Rustenberg, Stellenbosch, South Africa, 14.5% abv**
Majestic, £12.49

Rustenberg is one of the most impressive, consistent, and fairly priced operations in Stellenbosch for both reds and whites. This one is a five-grape blend from the big red stable. Dense, earthy, dusty, rocky almost, but hiding inside the mineral shroud is good, ripe but dry blackcurrant and black plum fruit. It's a bit of a beast at the moment, but its heart's in the right place, so enjoy its burly beauty now or allow it to become scented and soft in 5–10 years.

26 **2009 Cabernet Sauvignon-Merlot, Moda, Joseph, Primo Estate, McLaren Vale, South Australia, 15% abv**
AustralianWineCentre.co.uk, £30

Remarkable wine, a thrilling hybrid of old Italian habits and modern Australian know-how. Joe Grilli is one of South Australia's most talented winemakers, and he's of Italian descent. Here he uses an old north-east Italian method of drying the grapes before fermenting them.

This reduces the volume, increases the sugar and density of flavour, but also adds a brilliant kind of sweet-sour uncertainty, which means every vintage of Moda ages quite differently to the one before – but they all do age, superbly. This is still earthy, with a grape-skin graininess and bitter black chocolate depth, with the fruit showing as dates, dried figs and prunes. For a thonking great mouthful, drink it now; but keep it for 10 years and it will emerge as one of Australia's greatest red wine experiences.

27 2008 Riesling, Réserve, Trimbach, Alsace, France, 13% abv
♀ Great Western Wine, £17.70

The Trimbach family are intellectual, friendly, but reserved, and the wines have the same sense of restraint. That suits Riesling brilliantly; it's not supposed to make come-hither crowd-pleasers. This wine isn't too haughty. In fact its texture is relatively soft, with a slight meat-paste savoury smoothness, and maybe a lick of honey, but its real personality is lime zest, green apple, that strange but seductive aroma of petrol and a streak of minerality that borders on the ascetic.

28 2010 Chablis, Domaine Vincent Dampt, Burgundy, France, 12.5% abv
♀ Corney & Barrow, £13.99

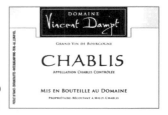

All the way through Burgundy, white wines are becoming rounder, plumper, softer. But I really don't want my Chablis to be soft. I want it to be mineral, to have a lean acidity that nips my gums. I do not want it to be creamy, as many current versions are. Well, Dampt shows how to be modern, yet true to the traditions of Chablis. The wine has loads of minerals crumbling like chalky earth through the glass, it has bright, lemony acidity, crisp green apple fruit and a few half-visible flecks of honey. Refreshing, pure, appetizing Chablis.

29 2009 St-Véran, En Crèches, Daniel & Martine Barraud, Burgundy, France, 13% abv
♀ Lea & Sandeman, £15.95

St-Véran is a sort of understudy for Pouilly Fuissé – traditionally the fattest of all the great Burgundies – and this example has learnt its lines well while throwing in a few of its own moves. This isn't a typical mainstream wine. It's pretty wild as well as rich. Honeybread mixes it with Christmas nuts, uncooked pastry dough, loft-aged quince and medlar fruit and that chewy acidity that is all that's left of orchard freshness in an old, dried-out green apple skin.

30 2009 Semillon, Tim Adams, Clare Valley, South Australia, 12% abv
♀ AustralianWineCentre.co.uk, Tesco, £11.25

One of my perennial favourites, just a little less expressive than usual this year, but still a class act. Nutty, savoury, with some spicy oak scent dappling the waxy leather promise of things to come, the custard and demerara richness which you'll get if you wait, the greengage-skins acidity and the honeysuckle that's keeping the wine fresh and bright for now.

31 2008 St-Chinian, Clos de Bijou, Domaine du Météore, Languedoc-Roussillon, France, 14% abv
♟ Stone, Vine & Sun, £9.50

St-Chinian is a lovely village perched under the wild rocks of the Montagne Noire in southern France. Most of its wines have vivid flavours, and this one's got a slightly shocking aroma, as though someone had splashed in some raspberry vinegar, but that's probably the Mourvèdre and Carignan grapes – they always add something rustic or feral to a blend. In the mouth, the richness is more of blackberries and licorice, with pepper and herbs tempering the ripeness before cinnamon and ginger spice fight back, only to leave a bitter sweetness of blackberry pips between your teeth, and the curious sweet sourness of rhubarb in syrup.

32 2006 Gigondas, Cuvée Tradition, Moulin de la Gardette, Rhône Valley, France, 14.5% abv
Booths, £17.49

Classic Gigondas, showing all the power and flavour of grapes broiled on the Rhône Valley hillside and almost baked by the sunstruck heat of the great stones and rocks in the vineyard. It's warm and rich and very true to brawny type, yet you can see the fruit in there, not shrivelled, a little stewed, but that's OK for ripe red cherries and strawberries. And hanging over the glass like a vapour is the heady aroma of the arid hillside's herbs.

33 2009 Riesling, Gaisberg, Birgit Eichinger, Kamptal, Austria, 12.5% abv
armit, £15.99

It's easy to forget that Austria is one of Europe's great wine countries because we see few of the wines over here. The Germanic labels don't help, since many of us struggle with the subliminal suggestion of Liebfraumilch lurking inside the bottle waiting to pounce and poison us. But this has nothing whatever to do with Liebfraumilch. This delightful Riesling tastes of runny honey melting on lightly buttered warm brioche, and this is made more challenging by a taste of old, old peaches with dried-out chewy skin but still a little sweetness lingering in their faded flesh and a sense of brittle crumbly rock. Swallow all that, and you're then left with the delightful impression of a peach Danish.

34 2009 Albillo, Picarana, Bodega Marañones, Vinos de Madrid, Spain, 14.5% abv
Harvey Nichols, £16.50

This is one of the wildest whites I know on the market right now. The Albillo is scarcely a mainstream grape variety, and Madrid is hardly thought of as one of Spain's main vineyard areas. But put them together and you get a

wine that behaves like a cake shop kitchen: every flavour that comes through is immediately transformed into a cake equivalent. Banana bread, carrot cake and rhubarb and custard tarts – and you need to pile in quince and medlar, orange, apple and peach – oops, now it's tasting like a tarte tatin. Wild and inspired.

35 2009 Pinot Noir, Las Brisas, Viña Leyda, Leyda Valley, Chile, 14% abv
🍷 Great Western Wine, £12.75

Taste this lovely, elegant, mellow red, and it's difficult to believe that this vineyard region is just a few years old. When Chile plants a new region, it seems to leap straight into top gear. This wine has everything you could want in an affordable Pinot Noir – smooth, almost syrupy strawberry and raspberry fruit, gentle tannin and acidity, a brush of herbs, a harmless scratch of minerals. Is it Burgundy? No. Is that a problem?

36 2007 Cairanne Côtes du Rhône Villages, 'Les Chabriles', Vieilles Vignes, Domaine Brusset, Rhône Valley, France, 14% abv
🍷 The Big Red Wine Company, £13.95

I've never seen a cork stained as black with wine as the one I drew from this bottle – a thick, impenetrable sludge lay on the cork. But that's wonderful. Industrial filtration would have removed the sludge and a lot of the wine's personality besides. That cork showed that all the wine's goodness was still in the bottle. Even so, it's a beast, and my initial sniff told me it was surely too big and thick. Yet it isn't. It's so dense I can hardly taste it, yet it's throbbing with the heat of the brilliant 2007 summer and slowly a dark brooding beauty emerges of cocoa powder and carob, of dates and prunes and sugar crystallized inside a shrivelled raisin skin.

37 2008 Mâcon-Verzé, Corney & Barrow Selection, Domaines Leflaive, Burgundy, France, 12.5% abv
♀ Corney & Barrow, £19.69

If you think this is a little expensive for a Mâcon, well, perhaps it is, but this estate belongs to the Leflaive family, many of whose great white Burgundies sell for ten times as much. Perhaps this is where the inspired Marie-Claude Leflaive lets her hair down: this is wild stuff that might be too funky for a few of you yet send others into paroxysms of gastronomic frenzy. At first the flavours seem baked, and the acid seems extreme, but then an amazing transformation takes place – quince jelly and tarte tatin and flapjacks dripping with fresh athletic sweat.

38 2010 Sauvignon Blanc, The Ned, Marisco Vineyards, Waihopai River, Marlborough, New Zealand, 13% abv
♀ Majestic, Waitrose, £9.99

This shows how important it is to have somewhere to call home. Brent Maris, whose label this is, has been without his own winery until this year, and however loud you shout and bluster, however precise your instructions, wine made in a contract factory simply won't taste as good as you want. And it didn't. But Brent

knows what flavour he wants and knows how to get it. This is the first time the Ned delivers: dry but full, aggressive in its green pepper and lime zest attack, and just subtly enriched with gooseberries in syrup before the crunchy, juicy, green fruit acid roars back and speeds the wine down your throat.

39 2006 Côtes du Rhône 'Dame Noire' Mourvèdre, Vignobles Coste, Rhône Valley, France, 13% abv
♥ The Big Red Wine Company, £11

This is a red rarity, a Côtes du Rhône made from the single grape variety Mourvèdre – the awkward tyke of Rhône red varieties. It's almost always used just for blending, because it's prone to giving feral, wild, herb-strewn (if you're lucky) flavours, rather than much perfume or fruit. And it is pretty tannic and chewy. There's a whiff of farmyard meatiness, but this is swept away by an aromatic cloud of sun-dried hillside herbs led by bay leaves and thyme and leading to graphite and a hint of wood polish as the dark fruit stirs. It's a tough wine, but rather splendid. Get the barbie humming – that ribeye steak is pixillating in anticipation.

40 2009 Clos Lojen, Bodegas y Viñedos Ponce, Manchuela, Spain, 13.5% abv
♥ Harvey Nichols, £11.75

In the lost valleys of Manchuela, way down towards Valencia on the Spanish Mediterranean coast, they've been growing Bobal for countless generations, yet it's only very recently that they've discovered what a fine grape it is. You'd think Manchuela would be too hot for any sort of elegant flavours, but that's the joy of using a local grape that's been quietly getting used to the conditions for ever, rather than some international interloper like Merlot that goes into terminal shock when it feels the heat. This has quite chewy, grainy tannin, but has a heavenly scent like pine-needle soap, and fruit that sways between the scented pale red of rosehips and the ruddy-cheeked sweet ripeness of sloes.

41 2009 Shiraz, The Black Pig, Loom Wine, Clare Valley, South Australia, 14.5% abv

🍷 Virgin Wines, £10.99

The Clare Valley is one of the cooler parts of South Australia, and as so many of the South Australian Shirazes become far too heavy and cloddish to enjoy, the less ripe, more focused joys of Clare wines become ever more apparent. These wines have as much weight as you could possibly want, yet have all Shiraz's great traditional variety of tastes because the grapes haven't been baked to death on the vine. This is a deeply attractive balancing act between black cherry and black plum fruit as ripe as you could wish, some lush almost chocolate-toffee gooiness brushed lightly over the fruit and an evocative Aussie scent of mint leaves and eucalyptus gum.

42 2010 Sauvignon Blanc, Crow's Fountain, Traditional Bush Vine (Villiera Wines), Stellenbosch, South Africa, 12.5% abv

🍷 M&S, £7.99

Villiera has been lauded as one of the Cape's Sauvignon experts for a considerable time, yet, though I appreciated the tangy green flavours of the wines, I often found them a tad sweet. Clearly M&S have said, we want your best green flavours, and we want them dry, but not fierce. The remarkable thing about this wine is that the feel in the mouth is quite mellow, yet the flavours are eye-poppingly green: green pepper, cos lettuce, crunchy runner beans, green apples and coffee beans, with some lemon zest and summer earth too. There's a little spritzy prickle to keep them fresh, while the acidity soothes rather than nips at your tongue.

43 2005 Semillon, Mount Pleasant Elizabeth, McWilliam's, Hunter Valley, New South Wales, Australia, 12% abv
♀ Tesco, Wine Rack, £11.99

Hunter Valley Semillon is one of the glories of Australian white wine, yet it got virtually swept away by the Chardonnay craze of a generation ago and has never recovered its fan base. Mount Pleasant Elizabeth is world-class wine, unique in its style. It has a high, lean, lemony acidity and a cold mineral streak, but this is waved aside by an amazing bone-dry richness of custard and toasted nuts and butter melting on slightly burnt toast – a remarkable combination of the lean and the heartwarming.

44 2007 Heinrich, Shiraz-Mataro-Grenache, Rolf Binder, Barossa Valley, South Australia, 14% abv
♥ Halifax Wine Company and other independents, c. £15

All three great old Barossa grape varieties thrown together in one wine. Just as it used to be. The different varieties complement each other so well (the French know this: these varieties form the basis of Châteauneuf-du-Pape), and unexpected yet delicious flavours are created by their coupling. So the wine is raw-boned yet lush, awash with chocolate and fudge yet with a finely judged acidity, soft, soothing, red cherry and strawberry, and from out of left field, an invigorating splash of pomegranate juice.

45 2009 Montsant, Planella, Joan d'Anguera, Catalunya, Spain, 15% abv
♥ Old Chapel Cellars, £14.99

Montsant vineyards are the outliers of Spain's glorious Priorat region. Some producers try to ape Priorat's dense hyper-ripe style, some settle for a simpler, fresher style and some, like these guys, aim for the best of both worlds. The result is certainly powerful – the core of the wine is a coiling stew of raisin and muscatel, date and dried fig and leather. Yet despite being massively ripe the wine still retains a delightful freshness: I don't know how, but that secret is probably why I frequently prefer Montsant to the far pricier Priorat.

46 2009 Pouilly Fuissé, 'Vignes Blanches', Domaine Cordier Père et Fils, Burgundy, France, 13.5% abv
♀ Majestic, £19.99

Pouilly Fuissé is supposed to be the fattest of the great white Burgundies, and this example is playing its part with enthusiasm. It has a lovely plump quality, savoury cream, hazelnuts and syrup shot through with surprisingly vivid acidity. Rosy-cheeked, chubby, not trying to taste like Meursault, not quite having that remarkable oatmeal creaminess, but it does nonetheless bear more than a passing resemblance to a Meursault of the more portly kind.

47 2008 Shiraz, Lionheart of the Barossa, Dandelion Vineyards, Barossa, South Australia, 14.5% abv
♀ Oz Wines, £13.99

Dandelion Vineyards make a range of wines from parcels of fruit they buy in South Australia, and they're pretty much all good. This shows the Barossa in its best light – piles of dense blackberry, blackcurrant, and black plum fruit, and chewy tannin halfway between grape and black cherry skins, and some brooding sticky depth like Fowler's Black Treacle if you dare to venture that far in.

48 2009 La Voûte, Vin de Table de France, Terroir Océanique, Le Chai au Quai, France, 13.5% abv
♀ Laithwaites Wine, £11.99

This Chardonnay comes from the large, successful Sieur d'Arques co-op at Limoux, and for those of you who've drunk Blanquette de Limoux, it was probably

produced at this co-op. But for top wines like this, the co-op behaves like an individual domaine owner; here they've chosen various single vineyard wines, vinified them all separately, then blended them to achieve the best final effect – which is a nutty, creamy, toasty delight. Nuts are most in evidence – cashews, lightly roasted, maybe even salted – and they go very well with the ripe apple fruit and the almost peach juice fatness on your tongue.

49 2009 Visan Côtes du Rhône Villages, Nature, Domaine La Fourmente, Rhône Valley, France, 14.5% abv
🍷 Oxford Wine Company, £12.60

Visan isn't a well-known Rhône Valley village, but that can play to your advantage because the quality here is tremendous while the price is very fair. This is powerful stuff, black and tannic, yet it still has a delightful fresh scent, a whiff of herbs and deep blackberry syrup fruit, all wrapped in succulent oak softness. It's a big bruiser to drink now, but will age brilliantly over 5–10 years.

50 2010 Semillon-Sauvignon Blanc (Evans & Tate), Margaret River, Western Australia, 13% abv
🍷 M&S, £9.99

If ever you feel like trying something similar to New Zealand Sauvignon Blanc, yet different, Margaret River in Western Australia is the place to come. Semillon and Sauvignon both give really green flavours here, and blended together add weight and intensity, without losing the acute, focused, almost twig sap greenness, abetted by nettles and apple peel, coffee beans and a twist of lime zest. Sprinkle that with sun-bleached rock dust, and you've as dry and tangy a white wine as any New Zealand could offer.

51 2010 Picpoul de Pinet, Coteaux du Languedoc, Domaine des Lauriers, Languedoc-Roussillon, France, 13% abv

♀ Tanners, £7.80

Picpoul is an acid grape, often thought of as fit only for making brandy or vermouth. Yet in the tiny enclave of Pinet, in one of the hottest patches of southern France, right down by the Med, more and more delightful, bright, breezy Picpoul is appearing at an eminently attractive price. This is spring-like in its optimistic freshness, pure, mouthwatering, juicy; apple blossom mixing with ripe, crisp apple and greengage flesh flecked with minerals. If there were a 'no mucking about' award for simple delights, this would win it.

52 2008 Ribera del Duero Crianza, Viña Pedrosa, Bodegas Pérez Pascuas, Castilla y León, Spain, 13.5% abv

♀ Bancroft Wines, £25.30

This very famous Ribera del Duero is a much darker, denser wine than it used to be, and I think it's lost some of its allure in the process. It used to be capable of a pingingly pure blackcurrant flavour, but that's hard to find nowadays. This has buckets of dark fruit, but it's more brooding than of yore and the tannins grip on to your palate, telling you the wine would really like a few more years before you broach the bottle. Even so, the traditional butter and confectioners' cream richness of the oak makes for a pretty impressive mouthful, which will be even better in a year or two.

53 2008 Shiraz, California Road, Dowie Doole, McLaren Vale, South Australia, 14.5% abv

♀ armit, £24.95

This is the modern face of McLaren Vale Shiraz. Usually modern means fresher, more focused, brighter, but in South Australia's Barossa Valley and McLaren Vale it generally means a belief that 'more is more' rather than 'ease back on the throttle'. It's a style thing. If you go for big, brawny Shiraz awash with cream and coconut and spice, if you want your fruit superripe and swirled about in a hedonists' stew of dark rich plum flavours, if you want the result to leave a memory of browned shortcrust pastry, rich jammy fruit and a shower of custard and coconut – sounds good? – then this one's for you.

54 2010 Gavi di Gavi, Fratelli Levis, Piedmont, Italy, 12.5% abv
♀ Corney & Barrow, £10.99

Gavi di Gavi used to carry the dubious sobriquet 'best white in Piedmont'. Since Piedmont was home to a clutch of Italy's greatest reds and most wine lovers would barely pause for breath as they rushed through a pitcher of white on the way to Barolo Barbaresco and the rest, this wasn't a title to crow about, and the wines were generally thin and mean. But the white wine revolution has arrived in Piedmont. This Gavi keeps the scything lemon zest tang it always had, but has added a hint of apple blossom, more than a hint of apple peel acidity and orchard dust, and a real slug of just-picked fluffy apple flesh.

55 2010 Grüner Veltliner, 'Mitanaund', Elisabeth Hausgnost, Wein und Genuss, Weinviertel, Austria, 12.5% abv
♀ Nick Dobson Wines, £11.50

A lady called Elisabeth Hausgnost makes this. She calls her business Wein und Genuss, 'wine and fun', which makes me think I should look her up next time I'm in Vienna. This isn't a typical peppery Grüner Veltliner: it has a hint of spritz, good juicy green apple flesh squirted with lemon and then, wow, a touch of papaya, some ogen melon, is that wisteria? Intriguing. And, don't tell me, strudel pastry softness. I need to arrange a visit.

56 2009 Côtes du Rhône, Domaine de la Janasse, Rhône Valley, France, 14.5% abv
♟ Great Western Wine, £10.60

Domaine de la Janasse is one of the most successful producers of new-wave Châteauneuf-du-Pape, which sells for a shedload of money. But this is its baby brother, which sells for a fraction of the price while giving you a pretty good idea of the Janasse style. It's superripe, like the Châteauneuf, and it does have fig and date and raisin richness – but it also holds on to some plush plum and blackberry fruit freshness. It's got a satisfyingly spicy aftertaste, and the tannic toughness could be harsh, but it isn't. The mark of a good hot country estate that knows what it's doing.

57 2007 Merlot Reserva, Carmen, Casablanca Valley, Chile, 14% abv
♟ The Co-operative Group, £8.99

Beautifully direct Merlot, full of fruit and spice, not complicated, but very satisfying. Blackcurrant jam and classy Agen prunes that gently morph into red cherry syrup, a little earthy grip and some spicy smoke with a tiny suggestion of eucalyptus.

58 2009 Zinfandel, McManis Family Vineyards, California, 14.5% abv
♟ Stevens Garnier, £8.99

This comes from a pretty hot patch in a hot land. Yet Zin likes it like that. It's able to build up tremendous ripeness yet still keep hold of oddball flavours and unexpected zesty zip. This is packed with date and spicy toffee, it almost seems slightly burnt, like the browned edge of a rice pudding skin, prune juice seems to be in there too, but then a welcome apple acid freshness saunters by, sprinkling coriander seed for good measure.

59 2009 Chardonnay Heretaunga, Lone Range (Capricorn Wine Estates), Hawkes Bay, New Zealand, 13.5% abv
♀ M&S, £9.99

Chardonnay is New Zealand's semi-secret weapon, and though Chardonnay has been a little out of fashion recently, it's still a stunning grape – and Kiwi Chardie is some of the world's best. Full, balanced, self-confident, with delightful flavours of honeysuckle, oatmeal, peaches and apple, the effect is like an un-corseted Burgundy – similar flavours, but with a rounder, more hedonistic texture.

60 2008 Cabernet Sauvignon, Hollick, Coonawarra, South Australia, 14% abv
♟ Flagship Wines, £17.35

Coonawarra, way down at the bottom of South Australia, is often thought of as Down Under's top spot for Cabernet. Wines like this show why. It's big and serious, but with beautifully focused flavours – vivid blackcurrant and green leaf acidity dusted with chalky minerals and a sprig or two of herbs. Ideally, I might like it just a little less rich in the mouth, but the fruit is so good, I'll take it as it is.

61 2010 Sauvignon Blanc, Spice Route, Darling, South Africa, 13.5% abv
♀ Halifax Wine Co, sawinesonline.co.uk, £8.99

Spice Route has become quite a big brand, and what frequently happens as brands become more successful is that they start to lose their focus and personality and all the flavours that made the wine a success get dumbed out. So it's nice to report that Spice Route Sauvignon is the best it's ever been – tingling with nettle and green pepper and apple peel crunchiness, cut through with lime zest, yet holding on to a little apple blossom scent and a teasing suggestion of exotic passionfruit.

62 2010 Chardonnay, Averys Project Winemaker, Limoux, Languedoc-Roussillon, France, 13.5% abv

♀ Averys Wine Merchants, £14.99

Most of the south of France goes from pretty warm to bleedin' 'ot. White wines rarely thrive in these conditions. But there is one high-altitude cool area down near Carcassonne that has consistently proved to be white wine nirvana, and in particular has shown a real penchant for growing top Chardonnay – and that's Limoux. This is excellent stuff – ripe, fruity, nutty, all at once; some almost succulent peach and pear fruit is freshened up by good acidity, while crunchy hazelnut and fresh dairy cream keep it lush but savoury.

63 2009 Dolcetto & Lagrein, Heartland, Langhorne Creek-Limestone Coast, South Australia, 14.5% abv

♀ Great Western Wine, £11.95, Vin du Van, £14.50

What a great idea. Take two of Italy's best glugging grape varieties, yet ones that the wider world hardly knows, blend them together under a well-known Australian label and say: don't be shy, you'll love it, it's a Heartland wine. This has an almost exotic scented black plum fruit that hunkers down boisterously with cocoa powder, grilled meat and earthy grunt. And the wine's power is delightfully undermined by thin trails of pepper and lily stems. An Aussie red for the future. More, please.

64 2010 Albariño, Orballo (Bodegas La Val), Rías Baixas, Galicia, Spain, 12.5% abv

♀ M&S Wine Direct, £11.99

Lovely modern white, that classic Galician mix of lemon and apple peel, polished leather, aniseed and flowers drying in the brisk sea breeze, then stones and seaside spray and the eternal promise of another rainshower before tea time. These wines were made for seafood, and when the wind is off the ocean, you can almost taste the brine in the wine.

65   2006 Semillon (McWilliam's), Hunter Valley, New South Wales, Australia, 10.5% abv
♀ Sainsbury's Taste the Difference, £8.99

Challenging but brilliant white. Hunter Semillons are always bone dry. Sometimes a remarkable flavour of melting butter on toast very quickly dominates the wine. Sometimes these flavours take a lot longer to emerge. This 2006 is a slow developer – its amazingly low alcohol, 10.5%, tells you that. These always start out pretty lean. It is beginning to fatten up with custard and hazelnut and toast, but you've still got the more gangly tastes of lemon pith, wood bark, damp earth and the metallic shock of fish skin to negotiate. Adult wine? Certainly. Fascinating? Certainly, again.

SYRAH
Vin de pays des collines rhodaniennes

2009

66   2009 Syrah Vin de Pays des Collines Rhodaniennes, Jeanne Gaillard, Rhône Valley, France, 12.5% abv
♟ Bancroft, £11.95, Majestic, £9.99

This is such a joyous style of Syrah. The red wines of the northern Rhône all use Syrah and they can get pretty serious, but just away from the main

vineyards, in the hills behind the river, are numerous little plots of land that grow Syrah but which can't call themselves by a famous name or sell for a ludicrous price, so they don't try to tart the wine up. Instead, they make it the way they'd want it out of flagons for their Sunday lunch. This bursts with exuberant juicy red plum and loganberry fruit, cinnamon spice, the crunch of peppercorns and the fresh dust from a harmless rockslide up the valley.

67 2008 Montagny 1er Cru, Le Vieux Château, Jean-Marc Boillot, Burgundy, France, 13% abv
♀ Goedhuis, £16.80

Montagny has a series of first-class limestone-based vineyards that wouldn't look out of place a few miles north nearer the famous Meursault. But because Montagny is little known, few growers, until recently, had made much effort with the wine; most of it went to the local (good) co-op. That's now changing as new generations take over and sniff the great potential quality for top white Burgundy. This is an example: almondy, oatmealy, dry but full with a little apple and green peach fruit and lemon zest acidity, and an aftertaste like barely salted porridge.

68 2010 Arneis Roero, Marco Porello, Piedmont, Italy, 12.5% abv
♀ Majestic, £9.99

Very enjoyable modern Italian white from the red wine citadel of Piedmont. It balances full-bodied texture, fleshy orchard ripeness and citrus zip without any component being compromised. The greengage fruit and lemon zest acidity are aided by a tiny prickly spritz and a beguiling aftertaste like scented candle wax.

69 2010 Sancerre, Domaine Serge Laporte, Loire Valley, France, 13% abv
♀ Christopher Piper Wines, £12.68

Ah, real Sancerre. Not the neutralized, softened, entirely unmemorable overpriced white that usually parades under this famous name, but a wine with the flavours that made Sancerre and its zesty Sauvignon wines famous in the first place. This is a prime example of how to achieve ripe flavours without losing Sauvignon's appetizing greenness. It isn't an 'in yer face' New World style, but the flavours are all there – nettles, green peppers, gooseberries, pebbles and sweet green apples – in more subtle Old World combinations.

70   2007 Santa Cecilia, Planeta, Sicily, Italy, 14% abv
♥ Great Western Wine, £19.95

Sicily is becoming one of my favourite red wine areas of Italy, and Nero d'Avola, its leading grape, is definitely becoming one of my top red varieties in Italy and beyond. What makes it so special is its ability to display unbelievable juicy, unctuous blackberry and blueberry fruit despite being grown under the relentless southern sun. This is almost wobbling with blackberry jelly richness, but it does have a nice chewy tannin to give it some gravitas and it is streaked with surprising floral scents like the stems of lilies and a syrup made of geranium leaves.

71   2009 Malbec, Altivo, Vineyard Selection, Finca Eugenio Bustos, Mendoza, Argentina, 13.5% abv
♥ Christopher Piper Wines, £8.69

Bustos makes two Malbecs. This one manages to be very ripe and slightly blustering in style and yet retains brightness and freshness. It's got some tough tannin but that's amply balanced out by heady oak spice and orchard scent that opens out into a bright, fresh mix of blackberry, plums and fresh cream.
• They also make a single-vineyard 'Secret' Malbec (£19.65), which is deep, dark, excellent stuff. But the bottle is so heavy and ecologically unsound, you'll have to make up your mind whether you're prepared to buy it or not, at the risk of jacking up global warming and giving yourself a hernia at the same time.

72 2007 BCrux, O. Fournier, Uco Valley, Mendoza, Argentina, 15% abv

▼ Butlers Wine Cellar, D Byrne, S H Jones, c.£15.50

José Manuel Ortega makes rich, succulent reds in Spain, Chile and Argentina; they are significantly different, following the dictates of the local climate and the quite different grape varieties. But his Spanish blood shows here. He has located some old but unwanted Tempranillo vines and has based this blend on their impressive grapes. Deep, dark plum and prune fruit fill your mouth, chocolate coats your tongue and tannin struggles to break through the lush texture, yet somehow it all stays in balance.

73 2009 Dankbarkeit Weiss, Josef Lentsch, Burgenland, Austria, 12.5% abv

♀ Nick Dobson Wines, £9.90

Lovely, sultry blend of three fairly full-bodied white grapes, in particular the Neuberger, whose only usual claim to fame is as the source of a few pretty syrupy super-sweet stickies. Here it adds a lush, fat texture, and it's difficult to tell which grape is contributing most to the flavour. The wine is scented with a pale green blossom, then drenched in peach and pear and honeysuckle syrup but pulled up short of being too indulgent by a greengage and white peach skin rasp like a cat's tongue on your cheek.

74 2008 Chablis, Domaine William Fèvre, Burgundy, France, 12.5% abv

♀ Bordeaux Index, £14.76

Fèvre is quite a big producer nowadays. But it is also one of the most consistent Chablis producers, so the fact that the wines are widely available, particularly in bars and restaurants, is no bad thing. This is honeyed, scratched with chalky stone, and sharpened up by a squirt of lemon. Spot on Chablis.

75 2009 Chardonnay, Odyssée, Château Rives-Blanques, Limoux, Languedoc, France, 14% abv
♀ Great Western Wine, £12.95

Cool-climate Chardonnay elegance, from southern France's most effective white wine area, Limoux. This is full of fruit – banana, apple and white peach – but it's dry, not tropical, and it even has a slightly chewy bitter edge. But that edge is invigorating in a Chardonnay and keeps the spice and the fruit very much on the refreshing side of the spectrum.

76 2010 Sauvignon Blanc, Urlar, Gladstone, New Zealand, 14% abv
♀ Great Western Wine, £11.35

Gladstone is one of the newest vineyard areas in the North Island of New Zealand, near Wellington. As such, Gladstone producers are dead keen to make their mark, and their wines are not for the faint-hearted. These guys could have made the Sauvignon leafy, lime zesty, tasting of gooseberries and green apples, but they went for the much more challenging road of trying to create passionfruit flavours. And that also brings in its wake a fair amount of grapefruit acid and an entirely typical whiff of sweat. It seems passionfruit and sweat closely resemble each other. Did you know that? No, nor me. As I said, not for the faint-hearted.

77 2010 Vernaccia di San Gimignano, Tenuta Le Calcinaie, Tuscany, Italy, 12.5% abv
♀ Goedhuis, £11

Vernaccia di San Gimignano is frequently one of the most overrated wines in Italy, but this example is lovely. It's another of those splendidly paradoxical Italian whites, very dry, yet seeming fat, yet also tasting lean and zesty and sporting a surprisingly attractive bitterness like orange peel and almond skin. This zesty bitterness really does work, and tempers both the incisive grapefruit acidity and the fat juiciness of white peach.

78 2009 Gewürztraminer, Castel Turmhof, Tiefenbrunner, Alto Adige, Italy, 14.5% abv

Majestic, £19.99

This is heavenly stuff. It comes from some of Italy's most beautiful vineyards, high up in the Dolomites towards the Austrian border, which is where the Gewürztraminer grape originates – in the Tyrolean village of Tramin. Clearly it loves its mountain home: this is wonderfully pure, crystal clear as mountain air, crisp and cool, and yet we're talking about a wine that's draped in sensuality and heavy-lidded perfume. That's its brilliance. Somehow this seductive mix of perfumed leather and rose petals, Nivea face cream and luscious white peach and black pepper has the fleshy indulgence soothed away and replaced by the limpid chill air of the high mountain passes.

79 2006 Rosso Toscana, Le Cupole, Tenuta di Trinoro, Tuscany, Italy, 14.5% abv

Corney & Barrow, £25.99

If I had to blind taste this, I'm absolutely certain I'd never put it in Tuscany. It's a delicious drink, but its overbearing impression is of raisins: lovely, scented, lush raisins. The wine is bone dry, but it's as though they kept every single grape out there to wither in the sun before squeezing out what juice was left into the vat to make this fascinating brew. I'm sure it's what they intended. I just felt I should warn you before you went out and thought you'd be buying some kind of austere, high-flying Chianti.

80 2009 Malbec Reserva, Viñalba, Luján de Cuyo-Mendoza, Argentina, 15% abv
♟ Majestic, £10.99

I don't drink Malbec if I'm in a contemplative mood. I drink it when I want to indulge, want to wake up my senses and treat my sybaritic side. In which case, this almost delivers. It does have a tremendous rich, syrupy flavour of dark damsons and plums all swirling in a cauldron of hot beef soup. But the French producer has managed to introduce a cautionary note to the party, a hint of Huguenot austerity and self-restraint that actually makes this Malbec a much better drink.

81 2010 Zephyr Sauvignon Blanc (Glover Family Vineyards), Marlborough, New Zealand, 14.5% abv
♀ M&S Wine Direct, £10.99

Just what I want Kiwi Sauvignon to be – bursting with the freshness of crisp, juicy cooking apples, zinging with the tart resinous delight of lemon zest, scented with blackcurrant leaf greenness and fresh-ground coffee beans, and dabbed with soft summer earth to temper the banner-waving, palate-cleansing acidity. Ripper stuff.

82 2009 Brouilly, Cuvée de Tête (Louis Tête), Beaujolais, France, 13% abv
♟ M&S, £9.99

These 2009 Beaujolais are so good. Very few Beaujolais are brilliant both young and mature. The trouble is, this wine is so ludicrously attractive now, which of you can honestly say you're prepared to shove it under the stairs for five years? And if you want to lose yourself in a swirling, head-spinning, magic maelstrom of strawberries and raisins, peaches and the clink of stones, held together by the chewy greenness of vine stems as a cloud of milk chocolate begins to form in the distance, straddling exuberant youth with the promise of something more mellow and lush – well, who's stopping you?

83 2007 Cabernet Franc, Raats, Stellenbosch, South Africa, 13.5% abv

🍷 Oxford Wine Company, £18.90

Powerful stuff, but not in the overbearing way that spoils quite a few Cape reds. Raats is famous for beautifully balanced white Chenin Blanc. Cabernet Franc is the only red he makes, and he's majored on the variety's mouth-watering fruit. Even so, there's loads of flavour here – rich raspberry fruit, blackcurrant leaf freshness and a cool, sharp acidity standing up to the smoke and stones and earth of the mighty Cape.

84 2010 Plexus, John Duval Wines, Barossa Valley, South Australia, 13% abv

🍷 Liberty Wines, Philglas & Swiggot, Noel Young, £21.99

John Duval used to make the great Aussie red wine, Grange. He now does his own thing, mostly with reds, but I'm particularly taken by his white. He uses a hearty blend of southern French grape varieties (Marsanne, Roussanne and Viognier) to produce a fascinating wine, harking back to the past more than looking to the future, its flavours autumnal not spring-like, its textures thoughtful and mellow, not crisp and meadowbright.

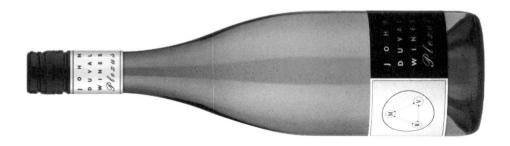

The apples are golden and kept a week too long in the pantry, the quinces are ready to be boiled into jelly, the goldengages starting to weep sugar and wait for the wasps. Wrap this in leather; wax the leather. Drink it solemnly – or keep it five years to see what it really wants to tell you.

85   2009 Zweigelt, Altenriederer, Wagram, Austria, 14% abv
Nick Dobson Wines, £10

Zweigelt is a smashing Austrian grape. If it had a French name we'd probably lap it up and it would be a drinkers' darling. But having a German name at the moment condemns a wine to pleading with wine lovers just to give it a chance. Well, I'll do the pleading this time. This is about as crunchy as a red wine gets. Crunchy as in celery, as in white peppercorns, and this gives a mouth-watering chewy rasp to the full red plum fruit and a mellow softness like red cherry shortbread. Full of fruit, savoury and scented with lovage, as chewy as grape skins, as juicy as the blood red grape itself.

86   2009 Bourgogne Chardonnay, Vieilles Vignes, Nicolas Potel, Burgundy, France, 12% abv
Majestic, £11.99

White Burgundy is one of the most ethereal, paradoxical yet utterly beguiling flavours in white wine. This isn't as lush and succulent as a top name like Meursault or Puligny-Montrachet might be, but all the dreamy white Burgundy flavours are there: hazelnuts, oatmeal, beeswax, rice pudding cream, crisp apple acid and stony dryness – but they're put together in a restrained way. If you age it a few years, all the flavours will have rounded out.

87 2008 Viognier, Breaux Vineyards, Virginia, USA, 13.8% abv
♀ Oxford Wine Company, £17.85

Recently, when I'm asked if I've discovered any new world-class vineyard regions, I'm quite likely to say yes, one of the oldest in America – Virginia. Especially when they grow the notoriously difficult Viognier grape. 2007 was a stellar vintage producing Virginian Viognier of unbelievable succulence and scent. 2008 made a lighter, milder, softer style, but this still has a delightful honeysuckle scent, apricot fruit and an appetizing dry texture somewhere between peach skin and scented leather.

88 2009 Pinotage, Delheim, Simonsberg-Stellenbosch, South Africa, 14.5% abv
♀ Wine Rack, £12.99

Pinotage is a grape that arouses fierce emotions, and this has caused producers to lose confidence in its delightful but truly different flavours and try to make it taste like Cabernet or Shiraz or whatever. Leave it alone. Let it stand or fall on its own real personality. This is bullseye Pinotage – quite rich, lovely mulberry fruit scented with rosehip syrup, softened by marshmallows still slightly smoky from being toasted on the barbie, and given a vaguely serious gloss with a haze of summer dust.

89 2009 Shiraz Reserve, Waitrose in Partnership with St Hallett Wines, Barossa, South Australia, 14.5% abv
♀ Waitrose, £9.99

St Hallett has a broad range of options in its large Barossa operation, and Waitrose has persuaded the winery to make Barossa Shiraz like it used to be –

big, mouthfilling but piled with fruit, not just oak and alcohol. This reminds me of why we liked Barossa Shiraz so much in the first place: deep black plum and blackcurrant fruit, some black chocolate and licorice to add both depth and an attractive nip of bitterness, and a surprising but altogether delightful whiff of mint.

90   2009 Crasto, Douro Red, Quinta do Crasto, Portugal, 14.5% abv
Majestic, £9.99

The Douro Valley in Portugal is where they make the rich, heady, insanely sweet Port wine, but some vineyards produce such thrillingly scented grapes it would be a crime not to taste their wine unadorned and sugar-free. Quinta do Crasto has some of the most beautiful vineyards in Portugal and this wine reflects the idyllic hillsides: the fruit is a heady mix of purple plum juice and blackberries swirled round with chewy plum skins and mouth-watering cranberries – and scented by a parfumier with drops of violet essence.

91   2009 Grüner Veltliner, Terraces, Domäne Wachau, Wachau, Austria, 12% abv
Waitrose, £8.49

These are some of Austria's most stunning vineyards – on terraces cut into the unforgiving rock high above the Danube. Grüner Veltliner likes these conditions and can produce fabulous flavours at pretty low alcohol levels here. A mouth-watering persistent acidity runs right through the wine, trailing in its wake dry but tasty apple and peach flesh fruit, the chewy greenness of grape stems, a suggestion of dry cream and a flurry of sun-warmed stones and dust.

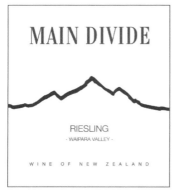

92 **2009 Riesling, Main Divide, Pegasus Bay, Waipara, New Zealand, 11.5% abv**

♀ Majestic, £12.49

The couple who run Pegasus Bay make some of New Zealand's most inspiring reds and whites, but Riesling is a particular obsession of theirs. They make it in every style, from puritanically dry to gum-bendingly rich. This one's on the dry side, but there's definitely some seductive sugar still left in the wine – a sweetness like crystallized sultanas or just the simple sweetness of the grape itself. Add the succulence of juicy peaches and a bouncy, zesty acidity sprinkled with salt of all things – and the result is a delight.

93 2010 Riesling Kabinett, Ürziger Würzgarten, Dr Loosen, Mosel, Germany, 7.5% abv

♀ Booths, T & W Wines, Waitrose, £13.99

Because Germany is so far north, vines struggle to ripen their crop and the position of the vineyard with regard to maximizing its exposure to the sun is of paramount importance. The Würzgarten – spice garden – vineyard is cradled by a sun-soaked bend in the Mosel river, and the glory of this Kabinett style of wine is that you catch all the golden flavour of the sun but never lose the soaring acidity of the far north. Honey is dripping from this wine, but it drips across tresses of limes and a cold, glinting surface of slate. Squeeze the lime, crunch into a green apple, sprinkle the honey with angel dust.

94 2008 Priorat, Humilitat, Christophe Brunet & Franck Massard, Vinoamory Fantasia, Catalunya, Spain, 14.5%
🍷 Great Western Wine, £15.80

Priorat was just about defunct a generation or so ago, and it was only the arrival of a bunch of revolutionaries aware of the potential of this wild bedlam of dark, rocky slopes that saved, then recreated, Priorat's greatness. This wine does flirt with modernity and freshness, but doesn't take it too far. It's still dark and stewy, almost thick on the tongue, with the bitterness of the burnt bits on an overcooked jam tart. But it also has the spice of an old Christmas cake and the slightly sweet and sour acidity of balsamic vinegar

95 2008 Pinot Noir, Domain Road Vineyard, Central Otago, New Zealand, 14% abv
🍷 S H Jones, £17.99

Central Otago is an extreme vineyard area: New Zealand's only desert, capable of being both hotter and colder than any other New Zealand region, so its wines are often marked by a certain pungency and attack. This Pinot is a milder interpretation, lightly spiced with the scents of the kitchen store cupboard, but any more than a light dusting would be too much for the soft, strawberries-in-syrup fruit and the pleasantly custardy oak. Classy, in subdued mood.

96 2008 Old Vine Zinfandel, Van Ruiten, Lodi, California, 15.5% abv
♟ Laithwaites Wine, £14.99

Lodi is one of the areas of California we are going to be hearing more of. It's a fairly warm area, and Zinfandel is the traditional red wine here – it's thought of as California's original vine. It makes heart-warming rich red vines that burst with flavour, but aren't in any way heavy: this one has a ripe, indulgent flavour of dates and dried figs, chocolate brownies and singed jam, but it isn't thick or dense, and even has a flicker of fresh acid running through it.

97 2010 Savagnin, Springhill, Irvine, Eden Valley, South Australia, 12% abv
♀ Vin du Van, £14.25

Savagnin (not Sauvignon Blanc) didn't arrive in Australia on purpose. Since it makes one of Europe's most unassailable wines – the shockingly rich-sour vin jaune – in France's Jura mountains, no one would have

ordered some cuttings on purpose. But a batch turned up, innocently labelled as Albariño, and was given vineyard space and I'm sort of glad. The flavour is not modern – it's autumnal and moist like medlars and quince, squishy with late summer rain, given some bite by green apple peel and pips, seared with the cutting, oily scent of lemon peel, twisted and torn over the glass.

98 2009 Riesling Kabinett, Piesporter Goldtröpfchen, Hain, Mosel, Germany, 8% abv
♀ Tanners, £12.30

Tanners of Shrewsbury always seem to have an enticing selection of German Mosels and of Spanish sherries – two wines just made for calm, reflective drinking after not too hard a day's work. Goldtröpfchen

means 'little golden drops' and is a magically positioned vineyard on the Mosel river, famous for making featherlight but honey-succulent, mellow yet refreshing whites. This is soft – all Goldtröpfchen wines are – but it's an irresistible softness of pastry dough and confectioners' cream, dipped in honey, and a subtle acid does ripple through the wine, and the cold rub of pewter-hued slate does chill it from afar.

99 2009 Minervois la Livinière, La Touge Syrah, Château Maris, Languedoc-Roussillon, France, 14.5% abv
 Vintage Roots, £12.99

This is a good example of Minervois: less scented, burlier than it used to be, but supported by a big whack of superripe fruit and balanced enough to be a pleasure to drink. It's certainly super-ripe, bursting at the seams with prunes and figs and black plums coated in carob and chocolate, seasoned with brown sugar, but this is thankfully harshened by the rough rasp of herbs, then mellowed by the bright freshness of blackberries.

100 2008 Chablis (Brocard), Burgundy, France, 12.5% abv
The Co-operative Group, £12.99

Brocard has become a favourite producer for the High Street retailers because he owns a lot of vineyard land in the less popular – i.e. cheaper – parts of Chablis and doesn't try to tart up his wines. Dead straight Chablis, that's what you get, at a fair price. This mixes good lean mineral scent with chewy apple and peach skin acidity and a lingering honeybread tenderness.

50 WINES FOR £6–12

Because of tax rises, duty rises, weakness of the pound, the weather, the English football team – well, because of just about everything really – we decided to raise our top price in this section from £10 last year to £12 this year. The £9.99 price point was becoming a barrier that many retailers were artificially clinging to as everyone's profit margins got cut to ribbons, and producers and retailers felt the temptation to dilute quality for the sake of holding price more and more keenly. So we put our limit up to £12. Yet I remember writing last year that the £7–10 area was the most exciting battleground – or playground, depending on how you see it – for those of us who don't buy because of the gaudiness of the label or the relentlessness of the advertising onslaught, but because of the flavours in the bottle. If we're prepared to go to less well-known areas, dismiss puerile, overpriced brands with the disdain they deserve, and strike out a little bit into the unknown, the £7–10 area is *still* full of the most fantastic wines. Out of the 50 I've chosen, 45 are still under a tenner. I was going to ask you to consider paying a couple of quid more for some really lovely stuff. You don't have to!

• In this section you will find white wines first, then reds, in descending price order.

WHITE WINE

2009 Petit Chablis, Domaine d'Elise, Burgundy, France, 12% abv
Stone, Vine & Sun, £11.25

Global warming has changed Chablis from being France's most gaunt and bony white wine. Many current examples are positively smooth and creamy as vineyards ripen their grapes better each year. So Petit Chablis comes into its own. Petit Chablis comes from the least good vineyards in the Chablis area, the ones least likely to ripen. But add climate change, et voilà – good old-fashioned Chablis at a nice restrained 12% alcohol. This is lemony, streaked with minerals, not at all raw; it has just a hint of honeybread softness, but even in a boiling year like 2009 it is suffused with the chill scent of pale northern sunlight.

2010 Bacchus, Chapel Down, Kent, England, 12% abv
Waitrose, £10.99

2010 was a pretty good vintage in the UK, but the crop was very big – for the second year running we had a sunny Wimbledon and that's when southern English vines set their crop. The summer, however, wasn't very hot, so the grapes struggled to ripen, leaving the acid levels fairly high. This doesn't matter for fizz, but it does make still wine a bit more challenging. So expect the acidity to be quite high, but put it down to English vivacity as you enjoy the hedgerow scent, the juicy nectarine fruit and the lingering flavour of elderflowers.

• M&S also have a good English Bacchus at £10.99.

2010 Chardonnay-Viognier-Marsanne-Roussanne, La Vinilla, Signos de Origen, Emiliana, Casablanca Valley, Chile, 15% abv
Vintage Roots, £10.99

Beautifully full, rich, yet delightfully drinkable white blend from Chile's leading biodynamic and organic winery. Ripe apricots and cling peaches in syrup jostle with toasty, nutty oak and lively piercing acidity topped off with spices and the perfume of honeysuckle.

2010 Albariño, Viña Taboexa (Bodegas La Val), Rías Baixas, Galicia, Spain, 12% abv
Waitrose, £9.99

There are some lovely wines coming out of Spain's far north-west at the moment. Rías Baixas is the main area, and because it is cool and damp and can make fresh, vibrant whites it became super-trendy in Madrid and, frankly, rather rode its luck for a number of years. But now we're seeing the true beauty of the region and its Albariño grape. This is full, dry, with the scented rasp of lemon zest, the wafting perfume of violets and yet some chill scent like rocks and leather and pale marble reminding you of the windblown sea-swept cliffs of Galicia.

2010 Verdicchio dei Castelli di Jesi Classico Superiore, Pievalta/Barone Pizzini, Marche, Italy, 13% abv
Vintage Roots, £9.95

Fine example of a modern Italian white, boasting a variety of flavours in subtle nuance rather than hurling them in your face. This is quite lush, waxy, yet reserved, suggesting flavours of peppercorn, beeswax, leather and syrupy apple purée – just suggesting, mind you, nothing too flash.

2010 Torrontés, Finca La Linda, Bodega Luigi Bosca, Mendoza, Argentina, 13.5% abv
Bancroft Wines, £9.25

Lovely scented, sensual stuff. I couldn't find any acid evident in this wine, and yet it was delightfully refreshing and remarkably dry. That's the nuts and bolts of it, but the excitement comes from wafts of rosehip, lavender and peach blossom perfume, brioche softness and a surprising and very welcome marmalade peel bitterness.

2010 Fiano-Falanghina-Greco, Triade, Campania, Italy, 13% abv
Waitrose, £8.99

What a joy – three of Italy's sexiest white grape varieties all flirting together in the same wine. The vines

were grown on volcanic soils near Naples – pretty much everything is volcanic near Naples – and the result is electric, each grape showing its strengths yet getting on with its partners. So the wine is savoury yet soft and fat, dry yet scented, lush yet streaked with lemon acid. Juicy pear flesh, savoury dryness, decent acid attack and the scent of the skins of fruit on a southern Italian market stall.

2010 Pecorino, Sistina, Terre di Chieti, Citra, Abruzzo, Italy, 13% abv
Majestic, £8.99

Pecorino has been around long enough for me to stop making cheese jokes. It's one of a legion of long-forgotten white Italian grape varieties that are creating a revolution in Italian wine. This comes from Abruzzo – an area known for chunky reds and little else – and when you taste this mildly perfumed delight, you wonder where on earth the grapes used to go? This is a lovely, fat, soft style, with warm, gentle, apple and pear syrup, sharpened up with a little green leaf acidity and peppered with lily stems. 'Scented fatness,' I wrote. Mmm … me after a soak.

2010 Sauvignon Blanc Reserve, Tiki Ridge, Marlborough, New Zealand, 13% abv
Waitrose, £8.99

This wine is so direct, so upfront in its tangy, tingling green leaf freshness, it comes as a shock to realize that it's English-bottled – which means, of course, that you're greatly reducing the wine's carbon footprint. And the quality isn't compromised. The wine has the kind of vivid, tongue-tingling green flavours that made Kiwi Sauvignon famous in the first place: gooseberries, green peppers, lime, tomato leaves, cooking apples – this is why we went mad for Down-Under Sauvignons. Thank goodness some people are still making them.

2009 Sauvignon de Touraine, Le Boulay, Dom. Jean-Marie Penet, Loire Valley, France, 13% abv
Tanners, £8.95

Much modern Sancerre seems to have forgotten about the allure of crisp green flavours and become obsessed with softness. Luckily, just downstream on the river Loire, in Touraine, there are an increasing number of producers who will certainly offer you wine that is soft not raw, but which is also bursting with the green flavours that make Sauvignon so attractive – greengage plums, squashy green apple flesh, green runner beans and a leafy scent, like a leaf still damp after a midsummer shower rather than one waving in the breeze on a bright, crisp spring morning.

2010 Chenin Blanc, Fairview, Darling, South Africa, 13% abv
sawinesonline.co.uk, £8.79, Liberty Wines, £9.99

The crucial word on this label is 'Darling'. Isn't it always? Darling is an area of the Western Cape with excellent soils, some well-established vineyards and, most importantly in torrid South Africa, powerful cooling winds from the icy seas just miles to the west. Chenin can cope with warm conditions, but it much prefers cool. This is a delight – gentle white melon with drips of runny honey smoozing up to chubby, ripe, yet green apple flesh. It's lush, honeyed, but beautifully refreshing.

2008 Riesling, Asda Extra Special (Knappstein), Clare Valley, South Australia, 12% abv
Asda, £8.68

Nice to see Asda taking a punt on good mature Aussie Riesling. It may not be an easy sell – Riesling never is – but the flavour is tremendous, so maybe Asda's stocking it will spread the word for this flavour-packed dry wine – note that Aussie Riesling is *dry*. Lime juice, grapefruit zest, mineral dust and a touch of toast and butter softness makes it worth a try.

2010 Bordeaux Blanc, Château Bel Air Perponcher (Vignobles Despagne), Bordeaux, France, 12.5% abv   The Wine Society, £8.50

At this price level, Bordeaux makes better whites than reds. In fact, it makes much better whites, especially in the hands of an expert like M. Despagne. This has a come-hither green apple and greengage flavour, just streaked with passionfruit and grapefruit, but the texture remains gentle while the flavours are unashamedly green.

2010 Rueda, Orden Tercera, Javier Sanz, Castilla y León, Spain, 13% abv
Real Wine Co, £8.49

Mouthwatering stuff. Initially sharp, with the bite of blackcurrant leaf and grapefruit, it opens out into a much gentler flavour of greengage plum, soft fluffy apple, and a bright, breezy, lemony acidity.

2010 Rueda, Verdejo, Palacio de Bornos, Castilla y León, Spain, 13% abv
Waitrose, £8.49

Verdejo is often called Spain's answer to Sauvignon Blanc. Well, it can be, not only for its bright zesty fruit, but also because it shares Sauvignon's propensity for getting a bit sweaty if the winemaker doesn't pay attention. They clearly took this seriously at Bornos, because this is packed with bright green freshness, green pepper, green apple, runner beans and fresh cut grass and the enticing whiff of newly ground coffee.

2010 Gavi (Fratelli Martini Secondo Luigi), Piedmont, Italy, 12.5% abv
Tesco Finest, £8.29

Gavi used to be the rather acidic, apologetic offering of white wine in the red wine bastion of Italy's Piedmont. Now it's transformed. It's still acidic – there's a good sharp tang of lemon zest and cooked Bramley apples – but there's a depth to the flavour, a slightly waxy texture, and a scent of apple and lemon blossom made more fascinating by one of those L'Occitane soap scents I can never quite identify, but which just might be sandalwood.

2009 Côtes-du-Roussillon Blanc, Palais des Anciens, Vignerons Catalans, Languedoc-Roussillon, France, 12% abv
Tesco, £7.99

If you like your wine big and fat and unctuous, you don't have to plump for a whopper of a New World Chardonnay: head for France's far south, nestled up against the Pyrenees, where ancient grape varieties give you all the waxy mouthfilling experiences you could want – without wodges of oak and at a mere 12% alcohol. This is plump, chubby, with just a hint of blossom and orange zest scent and a rich texture but dry flavour of fluffy apple, syrup and a dab of toffee.

2010 Sauvignon Blanc Touraine, Domaine Jacky Marteau, Loire Valley, France, 13.5% abv
M&S, £7.99

2010 saw more good Sauvignon coming out of France's Loire Valley than any year I can remember. Hooray! France is finally fighting back against the Sauvignon tide of the New World. And not before time. As too much Sauvignon from places like New Zealand starts getting sloppy, we need France to reassert itself. Touraine is just round the bend of the Loire river from the popular Sancerre; it isn't so well known and you get more taste for a lot less money. This is gentle in texture yet wonderfully green in flavour – nettles, gooseberries, Bramley cooking apples and a sappiness like an underripe green Kent cobnut.

2009 Soave, Passo Avanti, Cantina di Monteforte, Veneto, Italy, 13% abv
Waitrose, Liberty Wines, £7.99

'Passo Avanti' means 'step ahead'. This wine is a Classico – in other words, it's from the best vineyard area – but Classico wines are not allowed to use screw caps, so the producers said, Well, we'll downgrade the label to basic Soave rather than compromise our belief in the modernizing screw cap. Let's take advantage. The wine's a beaut — gorgeously full and soft with the oozing juiciness of sweet goldengage plums, pears and white peach and a texture that is waxy, savoury and creamy — and delightfully fresh.

2010 Rueda, Verdejo, Quintaluna, Ossian, Castilla y León, Spain, 13% abv
Justerini & Brooks, £7.67

Ossian makes a completely different Rueda to other producers — round, softer, warmer — yet still with a mouthwatering prickle of spritz, and the gentle but pungent citrus scent of boiled lemons to go with the warmth of baked apple peel, summer earth and a suggestion of fresh farm cream.

2010 Côtes du Rhône Blanc, Domaine de la Bastide, Rhône Valley, France, 13% abv
Connolly's, £7.66

We think of Côtes du Rhône as the home of gusty red wines, but they get thirsty down there during their blazing summers and need to make a local thirst-quencher. Rhône whites aren't sharp or tangy, but they can have a lovely, satisfying, mellow quality — honeysuckle scent, fluffy apple and peach skin fruit — with a flicker of mineral dust.

• Domaine de la Bastide's 2009 red Visan Côtes du Rhône-
   Villages (£8.35) is a good, big, burly number.

2010 Vinho Verde, Quinta de Azevedo, Sogrape, Portugal, 11.5% abv
Majestic, £7.49, Waitrose, £7.29

We've become so used to screwcaps these days that we may not realize this wine is making a brave departure. It's screwcapped – and it's Portuguese. Portugal is the leading producer of cork and it is regarded as virtual treason in many sections of the Portuguese wine world to use anything but cork closures. Yet the bright, slightly fizzy, ephemeral nature of good Vinho Verde cries out for the neutral and totally effective closure of a screwcap. This delightfully dry, rock-dusty, water-white wine, with a flavour of unripe exotic fruit – peaches, quinces and pears – squirted with grapefruit and apple juice, and scratched with lemon zest, needs to be as fresh and pure as when it left the winery vat – and the screwcap ensures that.

2010 Viognier-Tamaioasa Romanesca, Scurta Vineyard (Cramele Halewood), Dealurile Munteniei, Romania, 13.5% abv
Laithwaites Wine, £7.49

Romania has got some of the great unsung vineyards of Europe. Famous aeons ago, but lost to the dead hand of communism. It has taken the bluff determination of a Yorkshire company, Halewood, to begin to

restore Romania's confidence and the vineyards' quality, and if wines like this keep appearing, surely we'll give Romania a chance. It's ripe, balanced, exotic, scented with floral talc, awash with juicy pear and apricot and kept honest with the rasp of peach skins and a handful of high summer dust.

2010 P X, Elqui Valley, Chile, 13% abv
M&S, £6.99

The Elqui vineyards are so far north they're virtually in the Atacama desert. They produce fascinating red wines from Syrah and Carmenère, and the growers there wanted to make a white with a difference, so they chose Pedro Ximénez, whose only claim to fame is as the source of treacly brown sherries in Spain. They must have seen something I didn't, because this is really nice: soft, with a creaminess like bread yeast and squashy yellow fruit – yellow Golden Delicious apples, pale golden peach – not in spades, but just subtly there.

2009 Torrontes, Pacha-Mama, Las Moras, San Juan, Argentina, 13% abv
The Co-operative Group, £6.99

Torrontes is such a wonderfully scented grape that I long to say it's the Next Big Thing. But I think it's usually just too much of a good thing to catch on in a massive way. Even so, in the last couple of years there's been a flow of Torrontes that are sensual, scented, lush and yet remarkably refreshing. This one is lovely and bright, and marries citrus sharpness with floral scent in a hauntingly delightful way: a citrus bitterness like the crunchy peel from Rose's West Indian lime marmalade and the sharpness of lime juice splashed with caster sugar, soothed with the scent of lilies.

2010 Viognier Reserva, Montevista (Boutinot), Central Valley, Chile, 13% abv
M&S Wine Direct, £6.99

No one ever complains that Viognier has too little flavour. Too much? Frequently. Just right? Well, it's a joy when the wine hits the balance between succulence and freshness. Lack of acidity is often the problem, but this example has a mouthwatering lemon zest and nectarine acid to go with lush pear and apricot flesh juiciness and a hint of mayflower scent.

RED WINE

2010 Sherazade, Donnafugata, Sicily, Italy, 13% abv,
Liberty Wines, Philglas & Swiggot, The Sampler, Selfridges,
Noel Young, £11.99

Ah, the delights of Nero d'Avola. Its astonishing success has revolutionized
Sicily's reputation and Sicily has led southern Italy's other regions to a
sunny upland of self-belief, from which we're all benefiting. This has
excellent bright but ripe red cherry and blackberry fruit, a decent nip of
tannin and snappy acidity, and the Nero d'Avola hallmark – gorgeous
blackberry sweetness lingering in your mouth long after you've swallowed.

2009 Chinon, Cuvée Terroir, Wilfrid Rousse, Loire Valley, France, 12.5% abv
Stone, Vine & Sun, £11.95

Cuvée Terroir: that should tell me what to expect – they've made this to reflect the earth, the vineyard, the
place. So I don't mind the tannic roughness. I love the pebbley rasp to the fruit, the sapping flavour of vine
stems, and I revel in the lean raspberry fruit, so dry and pure I can feel the pips getting stuck in my teeth.

**2008 Cabernet-Merlot, Vasse Felix, Margaret River, Western
Australia, 14.5% abv**
Morrisons, £10.99

I was delighted to find this in Morrisons. Vasse Felix in Margaret River is making
its best wine for a generation right now. Lovely pure blackcurrant, a scent of
herbs, a chewiness of nut flesh and a bright mouthwatering acidity. Snap this up,
everybody: that'll encourage Morrisons to stock more goodies.

2008 Primitivo, Polvanera 14, Gioia del Colle, Puglia, Italy, 14% abv
Adnams, £10.99

Wine right from the heel of Italy, a baking landscape that produces rich, hefty wines. They don't always work, but this one does: thick with the richness of dates and raisins, the sticky taste of plum jam on the edge of a jam tart, and the glowering intensity of Fowler's Black Treacle and Harrogate toffee. Add to all that the whiff of vaguely spicy sawdust and you've got some mouthful.

2009 Pinot Noir, Asda Extra Special (Wither Hills), Marlborough, New Zealand, 13.5% abv
Asda, £9.98

Very nice, delicate, gentle red. New Zealand Pinot Noir has become a really sexy wine style, so I'm glad to see Asda giving it a go and choosing a classy producer, the trendy Wither Hills winery. So enjoy the strawberry syrup ripe sweet fruit with its soft caress on your tongue and its smooth coating of oak and tell yourself that it's a bargain – you'd be paying a lot more if it had a Wither Hills label.
• Tesco have also got a classy Kiwi Pinot Noir at £10.29.

2009 Régnié, Domaine Rochette, Beaujolais, France, 13% abv
James Nicholson, £9.89

There's some fabulous 2009 Beaujolais around at the moment and lots of very good 2010 to follow on with when that's finished. Régnié is usually the lightest of the well-known Beaujolais villages, but this one's pretty beefy: it's ripe, rich, almost serious – in that you could happily age it for a year or two – but it still holds on to Beaujolais' typical joyous welter of cherry and raspberry fruit and orchard bloom, only slightly roughened up by the rasp of stones.

2009 Bourgogne Hautes-Côtes de Nuits (Antonin Rodet), Burgundy, France, 12.5% abv
Tesco Finest, £9.79

It isn't easy to source enjoyable Burgundy at under a tenner, but the superripe 2009 vintage helps and the well-connected company of Antonin Rodet will know where the good barrels are. This is quite testing, but it's the real thing, genuinely dry yet with fairly deep strawberry fruit and some attractive lanolin softness, which is roughened up just a bit by minerals and the dust from the bottom of a jar of mixed herbs. Texture is the crucial component in red Burgundy and this has it.

2008 Bourgogne Rouge, Domaine Gachot-Monot, Burgundy, France, 12.5% abv
Fingal-Rock, £9.55

This comes from the village of Corgoloin in the pretty smart appellation of Côte de Nuits-Villages, but you're saving significant money because the producer has only labelled it as 'Bourgogne'. It's dry, it's meaty, with a cashew nut savouriness and gentle dry strawberry fruit. Mellow, old style, but above all it has a certain Burgundian caress – that's the Côte de Nuits vineyards delivering – so if you feel like an old-style caress …

2007 Bordeaux, Lea & Sandeman (Carteau-Dabudyk), France, 13% abv
Lea & Sandeman, £9.50

Basic Bordeaux doesn't get in this guide very often, but there's basic Bordeaux – and there's Lea & Sandeman's basic Bordeaux. These guys have gone to a very good producer in the classy area of Fronsac and blended up a wine that is so ripe it's almost rich. This has the leafiness and furry tannic grip of proper Bordeaux, yet it has the ripe red plums, blackcurrants, the dryness of summer country earth, and the promise of scent if you open the bottle an hour or two early, which would make me think it's a very attractive Fronsac at about half its normal price.

2009 Malbec, Ique, Bodega Foster, Mendoza, Argentina, 14.5% abv
Private Cellar, £9.49

Good, ripe, lush Malbec, managing to be juicy and scented with just a lick of tannin and no suggestion of sun-baked overripeness and grapes turned to raisins on the vine. (There are a lot of Malbecs like that: luckily most of them head to North America rather than over here.) Enjoy this for its juicy black plum and damson fruit, its floral scent and light oak spice, and its sort of semi-corseted lushness.

2009 Coteaux du Languedoc, Pic Saint-Loup, Domaine Haut-Lirou, Languedoc-Roussillon, France, 13.5% abv
Majestic, £8.99

Big, black-dark wine. Serious and powerful when you first pour it, but leave the bottle open for an hour or two and you suddenly notice there's lovely sweet fruit hiding in there – red plum, strawberry, red cherry even – the blackness opening out to dark chocolate, and the warm herbs of the Languedoc hills beginning to glow in the glass.

2009 Côtes du Rhône, Château Rochecolombe, Rhône Valley, France, 14% abv
Vintage Roots, £8.99

2009 was a very warm year in France's Rhône Valley – so you need to like ripeness that teeters towards being overdone and flavours that can verge on the excessive. Somehow this wine manages to be OTT yet not unbalanced: it's über-ripe and packed with sultana, raisin and date-dark fruitiness, yet still holds on to a black cherry freshness. The vineyard is organic, and the vines are 50 years old – that always helps.

2009 Malbec, Ascencion, Salta, Argentina, 13.5% abv
Laithwaites Wine, £8.99

These vines grow in vineyards that are ridiculously high up in the Andes: about 2500 metres. And the same estate has now planted vines at over 3000 metres – the highest vineyards in the world. What this rarefied altitude does is give intensity and focus to the wine. Malbec can be soupy and rich, but not up where the condors soar. This is warm but not baked, rich but not raisined, plums not prunes, and its treacly depth has the grittiness of mountain dust to keep it appetizing.

2009 Grenache, Vieilles Vignes, Vin de Pays de Méditerranée, Domaine de Cristia, Rhône Valley, France, 14% abv
The Big Red Wine Company, £8.95

This may only boast a humble Vin de Pays de Méditerranée on the label, but Domaine de Cristia is a serious producer at Courthezon, which is as near as dammit in Châteauneuf-du-Pape, the stronghold of France's greatest – and most expensive – Grenache. So Vieilles Vignes (old vine) Grenache means something special here. It's big, beefy stuff, you can feel the heat of the vineyards, yet the fruit stays fresh – bright, fruity, red syrup-ripe with a splash of chocolate and no hard edges at all.

2009 Minervois, 'Plaisir d'Eulalie', Château Sainte Eulalie, Languedoc-Roussillon, France, 14% abv
Tanners, £8.50

Minervois at its best has a delightful floral scent hovering over its dark, rich fruit. Very warm years like 2009 put the perfume at risk and tempt growers to go for black-hearted behemoths. I can sense the grower's uncertainty here – instead of a floral scent, this smells of fig rolls and dates and heat – but Sainte Eulalie is a wonderful vineyard and its character fights through the richness to reveal plush, mouthfilling damson, blackberry and pain au chocolat with a welcome whiff of hillside herbs.

2009 Puglia Rosso, Anarkos, Racemi, Puglia, Italy, 13% abv
The Real Wine Co, £8.49

This is an excellent example of how Italian reds in the south are ridding themselves of the tyrannical shackles of Tuscany (Chianti etc.) and Piedmont (Barolo etc.) and starting to express their own fabulous originality. It's bulging with youth, it's soft yet tempered by a nice edgy bitterness, and it throws together the richness of ripe red plums and very ripe tomatoes with the scent of rosehip.

2009 Carmenère, Llai Llai, El Bajo de Totihue, Maipo Valley, Chile, 13.5% abv
Tesco, £7.99

Serious, quite powerful red wine that nonetheless bursts with the fascinating fruit flavours of the Carmenère grape. It's deep, it's quite tough to start, but slowly the richness begins to dominate – ripe sweet blackcurrant, licorice, black chocolate, the burnt jam on the edge of a jam tart, and just a hint of coal dust.

* The Llai Llai Chardonnay (£7.99) is pretty good too, in a lush yet restrained way.

2009 Ciconia, Touriga Nacional-Syrah-Aragonez, Herdade de São Miguel, Alentejano, Portugal, 14.5% abv
S H Jones, £7.99

Alentejo is the warm, sunny hinterland of southern Portugal, where any grape can ripen to perfection and the wines achieve a lush generosity, easy-going, full of fruit flavours, but not just juicy-Lucy mouthwash – these are serious wines. Ciconia has a definite stony, dusty dryness and the tickle of light tannic bitterness, but that doesn't get in the way of a scent like rosehips and a dark, almost syrupy, fruit like a soup made of blackberries and dates.

2009 Dão, Flor de Nelas Seleção, Portugal, 13% abv
Sainsbury's, £7.99

Dão can be a forbidding wine. It used to be Portugal's most famous red, probably because you had to wait about a generation for it to soften and become drinkable – if it ever did. Things like that made you famous in the old days. What makes you famous now is pleasure – and this Dão is full of it. It still has a bit of tough-edged seriousness for those who must have such things, but basically it's pulsing with plum and blackberry fruit, a lush texture halfway between jelly and savoury cream, and delightful floral scent sprinkled with rock dust.

2009 Gamay, Fontvel, Côtes du Tarn, South-West France, 12.5% abv
Virgin Wines, £7.99

Gorgeous, uncomplicated fruity red, barbecue red, casserole red, thirst-quencher red. Gamay is one of the world's best grapes at making wines to gladden the heart and quicken the thirst. This is juicy, full of bright red plum fruit mashed up with strawberries, then slightly coarsened by the rough kiss of streamside pebbles.

2009 Mourvèdre-Petit Verdot, 'Les Derniers Cépages', Domaine Sainte Rose, Côtes de Thongue, Languedoc-Roussillon, France, 14% abv
Majestic, £7.99

'Les Derniers Cépages' means in effect 'the last to ripen' and that certainly describes these two cliffhanger varieties: in cooler years you can wait in vain, they're simply never ripe. But 2009 was a warm year, and though the wine is austere, with a slightly frowning style, the fascinating flavours make up for that: serious

palate-rasping Bordeaux texture from the Petit Verdot, along with dark chewy fruit and a hint of floral scent; and the ripe red fruit and wild bitumen seemingly flayed by a mad herb-gatherer from the Mourvèdre. Age it for 2–5 years and it will all make sense.

2010 Primitivo del Tarantino, I Monili, Racemi, Puglia, Italy, 13% abv
Majestic, £7.99

Rip-roaring southern Italian red that also manages to be refreshing. Primitivo isn't a subtle grape and there's a touch of the caveman about this, but it is young, and its boisterousness will have calmed a little within a year – the riot of carob and banana, cocoa powder, black plum and cherry juice will still be there, just slightly better behaved.

2008 Valpolicella Ripasso (Casa Girelli), Veneto, Italy, 13.5% abv
The Co-operative Group, £7.99

If you think of Valpolicella as a bright, breezy picnic glugger, think again. When you see Ripasso on the label it means the wine is in effect fermented twice, and the result is a massive increase in colour and concentration. Now the wine is dark, meaty, rich – definitely – but it's like a kind of black syrup stewed together with the charred bits from burnt toffee. There's a whiff of gum and herbs too. Powerful now, in its gruff youth, it will sweeten and mellow with 4–7 years age.

2010 Touriga Nacional, Alentejano (Falua Sociedade de Vinhos), Portugal, 13.5% abv
Tesco Finest, £7.79

Touriga Nacional is often touted as Portugal's finest grape variety. That's because it's really good at making dark, dense, scented reds for the long haul in places like Douro and Dão. Yet plant it somewhere warm and easy-going like the Alentejo, south-east of Lisbon, and it shows a much more jovial side – lush, round, ripe, full of rich blackberry and damson fruit and bright floral scent.

2010 Malbec Viñalta (Domaine Vistalba), Mendoza, Argentina, 14% abv
M&S, £7.49

You can taste the warmth in this wine, the baking sun that makes the vineyards of Mendoza thrum with heat on drowsy summer days. But the Malbec seems to thrive on it. You can taste the hot stones of the vineyard, the sun-thickened skins of the grapes and the sugar-filled soupiness of their juice – but it's not overpowering, doesn't blast your gums, and even has a hint of floral scent.

2009 Tinta de Toro Joven, Balcon de la Villa (Bodega Covitoro), Toro, Castilla y León, Spain, 14.5% abv
M&S, £6.99

Toro can be a bit of a beautiful brute, packed with flavour but armoured with mighty tannins. So this is something of an achievement. It is dark as tar and engine oil, it is dense and muscular, but it isn't bitter, and through a haze of drifting battlefield smoke and the scent of warm stones, you can taste a luscious, rewarding soup of ripe blackcurrant and black plums.

2010 Shiraz, Pays d'Oc, Asda Extra Special (Domaines Paul Mas), Languedoc-Roussillon, France, 13.5% abv
Asda, £6.97

This is exactly the kind of red wine we should see tumbling out of the south of France, but which is all too rare. It's rich, it's ripe, it's oozing juicy blackberry and loganberry fruit while giving off a floral scent that might be wisteria, and just a touch of oaky spice. All of this, and yet it's mouthwatering and refreshing too.

AROUND
£6

For years, £4.99 has been the price barrier that supermarkets have fought hardest to preserve, forcing price cuts on producers and demanding 'promotional' payments that run into tens of thousands of pounds – all designed to aid their King Canute-like determination to deny reality and admit that good £4.99 wine just wasn't going to be possible any longer. With the welter of tax rises we've seen this year, and the 'inflation plus 2% duty escalator' being enthusiastically employed by the government, most retailers have raised prices of these wines to £5.99 or even more. Honestly, it had to happen. I know a lot of us don't want to spend more than a fiver on a bottle, but for many producers the only alternative to meeting those price points and satisfying the supermarkets' lust for profit was to go bust. I've found a few decent £4.99ers this year, but we'd better start getting used to £5.99 as the new £4.99.

• In this section you will find white wines first, then reds, in descending price order.

WHITE WINE

2010 Chardonnay, Cowrie Bay, Gisborne, New Zealand, 13% abv
Waitrose, £5.99

The move towards bulk shipping affordable New Zealand whites is gathering pace, and if this UK-bottled example is anything to go by, we needn't worry about quality. This is very attractive, dry but full of melon and pineapple chunk fruit and just a hint of spice. It comes from Gisborne, New Zealand's Chardonnay capital – and this tasty white shows why Gisborne got its reputation.

2010 Cortese Piemonte (Araldica), Piedmont, Italy, 11.5% abv
M&S, £5.99

There was a time when Cortese wine – often sold under its more famous, and expensive, place name, Gavi – was pretty much the only white you'd find from the red wine fastness of Piedmont in north-west Italy. It was usually mean, gum-grating stuff. But Cortese is playing its role in the Italian white wine revolution: the wine is still sharp, but it's not raw, it's got a light prickle on the tongue, an acid snap like lemon peel and a unique fruit flavour somewhere between leather and the Kia-Ora lemon squash I had when I was a kid.

2010 Falanghina, Beneventano (La Guardiense co-op), Campania, Italy, 12% abv
M&S, £5.99

Delightful, fragrant wine showing why everyone is getting excited about Italian whites – after ignoring them for 2000 years. It's got a scent like a dab of aftershave from another era – Aqua Velva, could it be? – mixed with a little ginger and heady musk. It may be scented but the wine isn't heavy: it's bright, full of juicy apple and pear fruit and tugged tightly together by good acidity.

2010 Pinot Grigio, Mátra Mountain, Hungary, 12% abv
Waitrose, £5.99

You may not thank me for saying it, but this is one of those times when I'm delighted the price has gone up. Hungarian whites have laboured below the £5 price barrier for too long. They're worth more, as this one shows. With a soft honeyed texture, white peach and apple fruit with just enough acid sharpness, and a scent that hovers between apple blossom, orchard leaf and early summer dust, this wallops most £5.99 Italian Pinot Grigios.

2010 Rioja Blanco, Valdepomares, Spain, 12% abv
M&S, £5.99

People in the know tell me it's really difficult to persuade most of you to buy white Rioja. But if you like bone-dry whites with tons of flavour, white Rioja is hard to beat. This has a brilliant flavour of Cox's Orange Pippin apple mashed together with a dollop of pear, and the chewiness and acidity of apple peel. So give white Rioja a go. You won't regret it.

NV Sauvignon Blanc, Ngakuta Bay, Marlborough, New Zealand, 13% abv
Morrisons, £5.99

A fairly big, slightly tropical style of Marlborough Sauvignon, but it's still pretty tangy – passionfruit and grapefruit slugging it out with much greener flavours of apple peel and currant leaf. This is UK-bottled – which shows you can keep the quality up while you transport wine 13,000 miles in a converted oil tanker. Well, container ship, anyway.

2010 Verdicchio dei Castelli di Jesi Classico (Piersanti), Marche, Italy, 13% abv
Sainsbury's Taste the Difference, £5.99

Verdicchio can be quite a heavyweight nowadays, but this is very fresh, with an almost spritzy tingle. It tastes delightfully dry, with quite lean apple fruit enlivened by the mild scented acidity of boiled lemons and the crunch of peppercorn.

2010 Sauvignon Blanc, Freeman's Bay, Winemaker's Reserve, Marlborough, New Zealand, 13.5% abv
Aldi, £5.49

I really hated the avalanche of cheap sugared-up Kiwi Sauvignon that appeared on the shelves a couple of years ago. Still, it meant that we knew Kiwi Sauvignon could be cheap, and since the quality has greatly improved subsequently, well, it would be churlish not to recommend the good ones. This isn't completely dry, but it's got loads of gooseberry and lime zest flavour and a texture and taste that remind me very slightly of Rose's lime juice.

2010 Airén-Sauvignon Blanc, Gran López (Jesús del Perdón co-op), La Mancha, Spain, 11.5% abv
Waitrose, £4.99

Airén is a famously dull white grape, but with imaginative handling it can turn out some pretty decent stuff. High-tech winemaking, and some blending in of the Sauvignon grape (and a little Verdejo too), has produced this gentle, soft white, scented with apple blossom and summer earth and tasting of apple, pear and a promise of orange to come.

• The red Garnacha-Tempranillo, Gran López from Campo de Borja (£4.99) is juicy and good.

2010 Soave, Vignale, Veneto, Italy, 12% abv
Waitrose, £4.99

If basic Soave is rediscovering its roots as a simple, fresh white quaffer, I'll be delighted. This has almost more fruit than you're paying for – juicy apple, pear and a slice or two of peach – and its texture is mild and soft with a hint of cream, yet it's thirst-quenchingly easy to drink at 12% alcohol.

• The Vignale Valpolicella (£4.99) is bright and juicy, too.

2010 Verdicchio dei Castelli di Jesi Classico, Moncaro, Marche, Italy, 12.5% abv
Waitrose, £4.99

Verdicchio used to be a bone-dry fish-dish white, but the new confidence in Italian white winemaking is demonstrating what an excellent grape Verdicchio is – ripe golden yellow fruit almost like baked apples and peaches, kept fresh with the nip of apple peel and a sprig of mint and Adriatic dill.

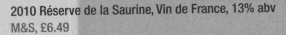

RED WINE

2009 Bordeaux, Château Gillet, France, 13% abv
M&S, £6.49

It's not often a basic red Bordeaux gets into my 'must-buy' list, but if anyone has developed a knack with cheap Bordeaux, it's M&S. And in this case we're talking about a decent individual property and a brilliant vintage – 2009. This combination has created ripe red plum and strawberry fruit and gentle toffee cream texture but has enough grainy tannin and haughty stony scent to keep it firmly in the 'needs red meat' Bordeaux sector.

2010 Réserve de la Saurine, Vin de France, 13% abv
M&S, £6.49

France's southern Rhône Valley is a good place to look for tasty reds at a fair price, so long as you avoid the big names like Châteauneuf-du-Pape and its neighbours. This wine comes from the less well known west bank of the great river and is bright, fresh and juicy, with very attractive red plum and strawberry fruit, lightly scented with hillside herbs.

2010 Bardolino, Recchia, Veneto, Italy, 12.4% abv
Waitrose, £5.99

The original bright 'n' breezy picnic red, Bardolino, from the shores of Lake Garda. Gentle, carefree wine, brimful of raspberry juice and Cox's apple flesh and the sharp reviving tang of blackcurrant leaf and lime zest. Serve it cool.

2010 Carmenère-Shiraz, Los Nucos (Luis Felipe Edwards), Rapel Valley, Chile, 13.5% abv
M&S, £5.99

Carmenère has a fantastic, utterly original flavour – but too many producers are trying to make it taste like Cabernet. These guys have gone all out for its rich, dark blackberry fruit and its delightfully off-beat soy sauce and peppercorn savouriness.
• There's also a plump, scented Los Nucos Chardonnay-Viognier (M&S, £5.99).

2010 Negroamaro, Terre di Sava, Puglia, Italy, 14% abv
M&S, £5.99

It's baking hot down in the heel of Italy, but the Negroamaro grape is used to the heat, and in 2010 ripening conditions were milder than usual, helping the grapes to keep their freshness. Even so, this is a fairly big beast – rich, a bit stewy, but with lots of bright, ripe, chewy and black plum fruit – but by harvesting early they've also kept some balancing acidity in the wine.

2010 Sangiovese di Romagna (Schenk Italia), Italy, 12.5% abv
M&S, £5.99

Sangiovese di Romagna used to be a byword for thin, raw red wine, just about acceptable to drink down with gobfuls of spag Bolognese. But change is coming: this is a round, soft, modern red, full of red plum fruit and toffee cream smoothness with a cautionary nip of leafy acidity and summer dust.

2010 Shiraz, Redbridge Creek (De Bortoli), New South Wales, Australia, 13% abv
Sainsbury's Taste the Difference, £5.99

This wine is made out in the parched hinterland of New South Wales, but 2010 was a bit cooler and damper than usual. This wine consequently benefits from rather attractive blackberry and black plum fruit that is a little jammy, but a little jam's OK, especially when accompanied by a whiff of smoky oak and a reminder of the parched dust of Australia's red heart.

2010 Vino de la Tierra de Extremadura, Spain, 14% abv
M&S, £5.99

Extremadura is way out in the wilds of south-west Spain and is still slightly Wild West country when it comes to sourcing consistent wines. But one of the joys of Spain is how previously unheralded areas are providing seriously good flavours at affordable prices. This one uses Spain's famous Tempranillo grape, and it's all about sun-soaked ripeness – no oak aging. It's powerful, intense, full of self-assertive youth, headstrong but very tasty, packed with black plums, tannin and prairie dust.

2009 Negroamaro Salento, Tenute al Sole (Cantine Due Palme), Puglia, Italy, 12.5% abv
Booths, £5.75

Big beefy stuff from the southern tip of Italy. It's hot down there, but the Negroamaro grape – that translates as 'black and bitter' – can cope. The bitterness manifests itself as a welcome peppery and rough rasp of herbs cutting across the dark, sweetish southern fruit, which nonetheless has good acidity and a splash of juicy blackberry.

2010 Garnacha, Calatayud, Cruz de Piedra (Bodega Virgen de la Sierra co-op), Aragón, Spain, 14% abv
The Wine Society, £5.50

If anyone asks where to find the juiciest, chunkiest, most rip-roaring red wine mouthful in Europe, I tell them to look out for Garnacha from eastern Spain. This is a gorgeous drink, bubbling with red cherry and bright raspberry and strawberry fruit, scratched affectionately with wild herbs, rubbed solicitously with smooth, warm, hillside stones. Top glugging stuff.

2009 Shiraz-Viognier, Douglas Green, Western Cape, South Africa, 14% abv
The Wine Society, £5.50

I'm continually puzzled as to why we don't see more examples of ripe, enjoyable, affordable reds from South Africa, so well done the Wine Society for sourcing this one, with its ripe blackberry and black plum fruit, its dab of exotic peach flesh, its trail of smoke and intriguing suggestion of orange scent.

2009 Tempranillo, Sabina, Navarra, Spain, 13% abv
Booths, £5.25, The Wine Society, £4.95

Navarra makes wines that stretch from the positively light and delicate to big brawny beasts. This is definitely towards the brawny end of the spectrum, but enjoyably so. It is a bit baked, but is balanced with attractive jammy dark fruit and a richness like Gale's honey dribbled on to buttered toast. Bring on the casserole.

2010 Cabernet-Merlot, Montgravet, Pays d'Oc, Languedoc-Roussillon, France, 13% abv
Waitrose, £4.99

Lovely red wine made from Bordeaux grapes grown in the excellent southern French village of St-Chinian – where they're technically not allowed. So the producers have to label their wine 'Pays d'Oc', which explains why the price is only £4.99, but the ripe, blackcurranty fruit flavour and creamy yet savoury texture is worth significantly more.

NV Chilean Cabernet Sauvignon-Carmenère, Valle Central, Chile, 13% abv
Morrisons, £4.99

This is so light and fresh that it could almost be a glugging Merlot from northern Italy. But there's a greater depth to its juicy fruit – without sacrificing the drinkability – and this plum and blackcurrant blend, just barely scratched with leafy acidity, makes for a good drink.

2010 Corbières, Réserve de la Perrière (Mont Tauch), Languedoc-Roussillon, France, 13% abv
Waitrose, £4.99

If you like your red wines full of fruit but packing a real punch, Corbières, down in the wild mountain valleys near the Spanish border, is still my 'go-to' place. The dominant grape gives a ripe but crisp redcurrant and red plum fruit, which in this case is roughened by hillside rocks, yet daubed in dusty chocolate.

2010 Rosso Piceno, Moncaro, Marche, Italy, 12.5% abv
Waitrose, £4.99

The glugging red of holidaymakers on Italy's sandy Adriatic coast. Some examples are a bit stringy and rough, but not this one. It's actually quite rich, full of a sort of red plum syrup flavour that is juicy rather than cloying and which is freshened up by the scent of pears.

2010 Shiraz, Dolphin Bay, Western Cape, South Africa, 13.5% abv
M&S, £4.99

Good, affordable, South African reds are not nearly as commonplace as they should be, but this one's pretty good. Full, fresh red plum fruit, some creamy softness to balance the acidity, and a sprinkling of rock dust.

2005 Viña Decana Reserva, Utiel-Requena, Spain, 13% abv
Aldi, £4.99

Aldi are very good at sniffing out batches of wine that have been forgotten in the dusty depths of the winery. You can taste the warm, sun-baked fruit in this, but it's got attractive spicy oak and a reassuringly mellow feel. Old-style stuff with a modern touch.

CHEAP AND CHEERFUL

This is becoming one of the toughest parts of the book to do well. Many retailers have virtually given up offering anything at under £4. Some have virtually abandoned anything under a fiver. So it isn't merely that there is less good, cheap stuff about, there's less cheap stuff full stop. Obviously you can blame the government with its welter of tax rises, but there is also a certain realism being forced on our retailers that fewer and fewer producers are able or prepared to provide wine at a sub-£4 level. Typically, Aldi is the most successful, but others, like Asda and Tesco, who used to offer a fair bit of good grog at under £4, now prefer to play in the under £5 world and accept that they will lose customers – customers they probably couldn't afford to keep. I've added 50p to our maximum this year – £4.50 and below is now cheap and cheerful. And I'm still trying. I'm putting my nose in the trough but pearls are ever harder to find among the swill.

• In this section you will find white wines first, then reds, in descending price order.

WHITE WINE

2009 Macabeo Blanco, Las Corazas, Vino de la Tierra de Castilla, Spain, 12.5% abv
Martinez Wines, £4.50

Macabeo is one of the world's more neutral grapes, but if you handle it carefully, it can produce some pretty nice mellow quaffers. This is almost waxy, very round and soft, with just a hint of honey to sweeten the mild peach and fluffy apple fruit. No massive personality, yet sufficiently succulent to work.

2010 Chardonnay, South Eastern Australia, 13.5% abv
Asda, £4.48

Australia is making an effort with its Chardies at all price points. I'd like this just a fraction drier, but it's a nice drink, mildly spicy and with just enough peach and apple fruit to keep it refreshing.

2010 Cuvée Pêcheur, Vin de France, 11.5% abv
Waitrose, £4.35

This has always been a good cheap white standby, but this year it's more like a stand-out. It's so bright and sharp, with scintillating leafy acidity and vivid greengage and green apple fruit. Why trade up when a basic is this good?

- Waitrose also has a good, juicy red Cuvée Chasseur (£4.35).
- M&S has a bright, tangy white Vin de Pays du Gers (£4.29).

2010 Soave Classico (Equipe), Veneto, Italy, 12% abv
Tesco, £4.29

Soave used to be a byword for fairly undrinkable party whites in screw-topped flagon-sized bottles. But properly made it is one of the most easygoing soft-natured whites in Europe, with vaguely waxy texture, slightly baked apple fruit, and a barely discernible streak of lemon acidity.

2010 Eva's Vineyard, Chenin Blanc-Pinot Grigio-Királyleányka, Hilltop Neszmély, Észak-Dunántul Region, Hungary, 10.5% abv
Waitrose, £3.99

Year after year Hungary delivers delightfully tasty whites at very friendly prices. Usually these are based on the internationally known grape varieties because the names of Hungary's native grape varieties are off-puttingly unintelligible for all but the locals. This blends international and indigenous – our old friend Pinot Grigio is in there – and has a lovely, rather original flavour of apple-peach flesh, a squirt of lemon juice and just a lick of some zesty green herb like lemon verbena.

2010 Pinot Grigio, Villa Malizia, IGT Venezie, Italy, 12% abv Aldi, £3.99

Pinot Grigio has made an unlikely name for itself as being the 'safe' white wine choice for those who don't want too much flavour but do want to show a little bit of class. There's a lot of overpriced dross on the market, but the Pinot Grigio grape can actually be rather good for the job. No one's going to go into raptures about this example, but it's pretty nice – pale, gentle, gulpable, with a dash of spice livening up its apple turnover fruit.

2010 Sauvignon Blanc, Cambalala, Western Cape, South Africa, 12.5% abv
Aldi, £3.99

South Africa's really making a name for itself as the home of zingy, tasty, wind-chilled Sauvignon Blancs further up the price scale. So it's encouraging to find some at the bargain basement end too. This is quite soft, a little softer than I'd ideally like, but it has decent leafiness, apple peel and summer dust flavours to compensate.

• The Pinotage-Shiraz (£3.89) from the same producer is also good – quite light, but with a smoky mulberry and marshmallow taste.

RED WINE

NV Shiraz-Cabernet, Virtue, South Australia, 13.5%
Waitrose, £4.49

Is this the face of the future for wines under a fiver – shipped in bulk and bottled in the UK? It may well be, and quality at this level needn't suffer if it's carefully done, while, of course, it uses a lot less carbon miles.

This is a very nice glugger, with fresh, blackcurrant fruit, a nip of tannin and an appetizing, almost lime-zesty acidity. Rather like Aussie gluggers used to be before the sugared plonk brands took over.

2010 Rioja, Marques del Norte, Spain, 14% abv
Asda, £4.23

You simply don't expect to find any Rioja at this price, let alone decent, drinkable stuff. This is a really good casserole red – and, in fact, its flavours are a little cooked, but that's OK. Stewed red plums, and some strawberry jam to fatten things up? Not classically Rioja, but then nor is the price.

NV Côtes du Rhône, Sainsbury's House (Union des Vignerons des Côtes du Rhône), Rhône Valley, France, 13% abv
Sainsbury's, £3.99

Just the kind of Côtes du Rhône you would be happy with in a village bar somewhere south of Lyons – pleasant strawberry syrup fruit, a dusting of herbs and spice, and fairly chewy tannins. Shove that with a platter of local charcuterie and cheese and it'll seem just right.

NV Corbières, Sainsbury's House (Les Vignerons de la Méditerranée), Languedoc-Roussillon, France, 12.5% abv
Sainsbury's, £3.69

House red and house white – it's such a good concept. We've all plumped for the 'house' in the bars and restaurants of Britain in the hope that they will match up to that old adage that you should be able to judge an establishment by its 'house' wine – so if Sainsbury's 'house' wines were no good, shouldn't I take my food shopping elsewhere? Luckily these are good wines, direct, true to style, uncomplicated, affordable. Spot on, in other

words. This Corbières is very fresh, banana mixing with soft red plum, and the Corbières mountain character shows in a brush of herbs and the rasp of peach skin and stone dust. Perfect picnic red.

2010 Shiraz, La Tinta, Bodegas López Mercier, Spain, 13% abv
Aldi, £3.49

If Spain can produce more fruity, mouthfilling, tasty Shirazes like this, Australia had better watch out. This is bright and fresh, ripe red plum and red cherry fruit just warmed up a bit by raisins, then cooled by apple acid and a hint of soft scent. Very good basic Shiraz.

2009 Tempranillo, Toro Loco, Utiel Requena, Spain, 12.5% abv
Aldi, £3.49

This is seriously good stuff for £3.49. The Tempranillo is Spain's most popular grape, but it generally likes to grow in conditions that don't resemble a Saharan hothouse. Well, Utiel Requena isn't quite Sahara, but it *is* hot, and it's some achievement to come up with this attractively direct style, with red plum and stewy strawberry fruit and just a touch of toast and spice – and bucketsful of drinkability.

ROSÉ WINES

I'm hoping that the idea of rosé wine being just a 'girly' drink is long gone. And I'm hoping that the idea of pink wine just being a fill-in when no one can decide between red and white is long gone too. And as for rosé just being sweetish, characterless sugar-water – well, there is still quite a lot of that about, mostly from the big boys in the US – there's never been a wider selection of really tasty pink wine, made from top-notch grape varieties in top-notch vineyard regions. Rosé sales have shot up in recent years, as more and more of us realize that good rosé is a great drink in its own right.

• The wines are listed in descending price order.

2010 Chinon, Cabernet Franc, Goutte de Rosé, Domaine de la Noblaie, Loire Valley, France, 12.5% abv
Haynes, Hanson & Clark, £10.15

This comes from Domaine de la Noblaie, a serious red wine producer, and to concentrate their red wine flavours and colours, they often drain off a little of the fermenting wine and make it into rosé. But you can still taste the quality of the red wine vineyard here – lovely leafy freshness, a fair old mouthful of ever so slightly jammy blackcurrant – and isn't blackcurrant jam simply the best? – and a marvellous texture, like syrup washing over ice-cold stones.

2010 Côtes de Provence Rosé, Château Saint Baillon, Provence, France, 13% abv
Goedhuis, £9.60

If someone asks me what's so special about Côtes de Provence and why it's so expensive, I wheel out this beauty. Texture, I tell them. Diaphanous pale pink, hardly darker than water. Flavours of apple and apple blossom sometimes with a distant suggestion of peach. And a sensation as you swallow the wine that glides over your tongue like silk and soothes your throat as it slips down. That's what you pay for. That, and the idle dreams of glinting Mediterranean seas, million pound yachts and the odd pouting starlet or two.

2010 Coteaux d'Aix-en-Provence Rosé, La Chapelle, Château Pigoudet, Provence, France, 13% abv
Majestic, £8.99

Château Pigoudet makes very serious, beefy reds, and this pink version doesn't stint on flavour. Lovely, juicy nectarine and Williams pear fruit oozes across your palate, teasing your mouth to water as it passes. Fresh, fruity, ripe and zesty pink.

2010 Côtes de Provence Rosé, Mirabeau, Provence, France, 12.5% abv
Waitrose, £8.99

Whenever I read that a wine-producing property in the dreamy, rarefied air of
Provence is owned by an English couple, I fall into a reverie of throwing everything
up and heading south to a vinous idyll. Ah well, another time. Let the Cronk family
take the risk. But they've minimized the risk by employing another Brit – maestra
Angela Muir MW – to make the wine. She's produced a lovely, juicy, peardrop and
peach-fresh wine, youthful yet creamily soft. Ah yes, sitting by my pool, gazing out
over the Med, sipping an ice-cold glass … yes, yes.

2010 Pinot Noir Rosé, Secano Estate (Viña Leyda), Leyda Valley, Chile, 13.5% abv
M&S, £8.49

Chilean rosés can sometimes offer you almost too much fruit and flavour; this one shows European
restraint. Appetizing salmon-pink colour, ripe strawberry fruit and creamy texture, with some apple
peel chewiness and a touch of savoury syrupiness – but all in pastel shades, nothing that would scare
the horses.

2010 Sauvignon Blanc Rosé, Southbank Estate, Marlborough, New Zealand, 13% abv
Majestic £7.99, Waitrose, £8.99

You probably think Sauvignon Blanc is called 'Blanc' because it makes white wines, not pink. And you
probably think of Kiwi Sauvignon as a green zingy blast. So shut your eyes and you get a great gobful of
gooseberry green leaf and green apple fruit. Open your eyes, and it's pink. Word in your shell-like. Add 4%
Syrah to the Sauvignon, gives it a lovely blush, don't tell anyone.

2010 Touraine Rosé, Les Cabotines, Domaine Joël Delaunay, Loire Valley, France, 12.5% abv
Stevens Garnier, £7.99

Touraine isn't the best-known part of the Loire Valley wineland, yet it is nowadays producing some of the best flavours at the most affordable prices. Delaunay makes tremendous, fairly priced reds and whites, and throws in this gentle, pastry-soft, mildly strawberryish delicacy to keep the party going.

2010 Pinotage Rosé, La Capra, Fairview, Paarl, South Africa, 13% abv
Co-operative, £7.50

Delightful stuff. I don't often use the words 'delightful' and 'Pinotage' in the same sentence, since Pinotage is a strange, curmudgeonly grape that scowls more than it smiles. It's smiling here, full of lively fresh appley fruit, snappy acidity, a slight scent of mulberries and a definite waft of smoky, nearly-burnt marshmallows. Which is just how the smiley Pinotage should taste.

2010 Nero d'Avola Rosé (Cantine Settesoli), Sicily, Italy, 12.5% abv
Tesco Finest, £6.99

Nero d'Avola is Sicily's finest grape for red wines. I'll rephrase that: Nero d'Avola is one of the finest red grapes in all of Europe. So when the Sicilians decide to make some rosé from it, don't expect a shrinking violet, because you won't get it. This is fresh, bright but deep, almost fat, with a whiff of menthol and a brush of herbs to sharpen up the broad strawberry and apple syrup fruit. Don't mess with it. Just drink it.

2009 Viña Sol Rosé, Torres, Catalunya, Spain, 13.5% abv
Booths, Majestic, Morrisons, Waitrose, c.£6.50–£7.50

The white Viña Sol, ice cold, is one of Europe's great thirst-quenchers. So I was delighted to see that the pink version has got the same objectives – lots of flavour, brightness and keenness to please. This is fresh, ripe, with red cherry and red plum fruit gee'd up by good apple acidity, and only a pleasing hint of raisin reminds you it comes from a very warm part of the world, Catalunya.

NV Grenache Rosé, Plume, Domaine la Colombette, Vin de Pays des Coteaux du Libron, Languedoc-Roussillon, France, 9% abv
Booths, £6.29

Very pale salmon colour, then a delightful, soft, mellow texture, so it comes as no surprise when the fruit is also mellow, smooth, the apple taste all soft and fluffy and the freshness helped by the merest chew of apple peel. What will surprise you is that this nicely balanced mouthful is only 9% alcohol. Slurp on!

NV Grenache Rosé, Vin de Pays des Coteaux de l'Ardèche (Les Vignerons Ardechois), Rhône Valley, France, 13.5% abv
Sainsbury's, £4.29

This bright but chubby pink comes from the hidden valleys of the Ardèche – a captivating lost region behind the much better-known Rhône Valley. It's made lovely wine for decades, but has never caught the public's imagination, so prices stay low but quality remains high. Plump apple and banana fruit, scented by strawberries, soothed with syrup – easy come, easy go.

Keeping it light

We're becoming increasingly disenchanted with high-alcohol wines. So, increasingly, I'm checking the alcohol content of the wines I recommend. Here are my suggestions for drinks with fab flavours that won't leave you fuzzy-headed the next morning.

More and more wines seem to be hitting our shores at 14.5%, 15% – even 15.5% abv. That's fine if the alcohol is balanced by ripe fruit and good acidity – but don't think of these wines as a jolly beverage to knock back with your lamb chops: you'll be asleep or drunk before you've got the meat off the barbie.

Now, some wines have traditionally been high in alcohol, and wear their strength well, but there are far too many wines that – less than a decade ago – used to perform at 11.5–12.5% alcohol and which are now adding at least a degree – and often more – to their strength, seemingly in an effort to ape the ripe round flavours of the New World. Thank goodness there are still a significant number showing more restraint.

At 12.5% there are lots of wines, particularly from cooler parts of France – most Beaujolais is 12–12.5% – northern Italy, where the most famous examples would be the Veneto reds Valpolicella and Bardolino and the white Soave, and from numerous parts of Eastern Europe, particularly Hungary.

But we've set the bar at 12% abv. This cuts out a lot of red wines; the slightly tart, refreshing white styles that sit easily at 12% can develop better flavour at a lower strength than most reds can. This exercise reminded us that Germany is full of fantastic Riesling wines as low as 7.5%. Muscadet is usually only 12%. Many supermarket house reds and whites are 11.5–12%. Western Australian whites are often 12%. And Champagne, along with most other sparkling wines, is only 12%. Hallelujah.

• VdP = Vin de Pays

White wine

- 2010 Airén-Sauvignon Blanc, Gran López, La Mancha, Spain, £4.99, Waitrose, 11.5% (page 89)
- 2009 Albariño, Eiral, Rias Baixas, Galicia, Spain, £13.99, Wine Rack, 12%
- 2010 Albariño, Viña Taboexa, Rías Baixas, Galicia, Spain, £9.99, Waitrose, 12% (page 65)
- 2010 Bacchus, Chapel Down, Kent, England, £10.99, Waitrose, 12% (page 64)
- 2009 Blanc de Morgex et de la Salle, Vini Estremi, Valle d'Aosta, Italy, £11.95, Caves de Pyrène, 12%
- 2009 Bourgogne Chardonnay, Vieilles Vignes, Nicolas Potel, Burgundy, France, £11.99, Majestic, 12% (page 55)
- 2010 Chardonnay-Sauvignon Blanc, Dom. de la Fruitière, Loire Valley, France, £7.99, Waitrose, 12%
- 2010 Chenin Blanc-Pinot Grigio-Királyleányka, Eva's Vineyard, Hilltop Estate, Észak-Dunántul Region, Hungary, £3.99, Waitrose, 10.5% (page 99)
- 2010 Colombard, La Biondina, Primo Estate, Adelaide, South Australia, £9.99, AustralianWineCentre.co.uk, 12% (page 22)
- 2010 Colombard-Gros Manseng, Côtes de Gascogne, Vignobles des Aubas, £6.99, Majestic, 12%
- 2010 Cortese Piemonte, Italy, £5.99, M&S, 11.5% (page 86)
- 2010 Côtes de Gascogne, Charte d'Assemblage Blanc, South-West France, £7.99, Waitrose, 12%
- 2010 Côtes de Gascogne, Les Quatre Cépages, Dom. de Pajot, France, £6.99, Vintage Roots, 12%
- 2009 Côtes-du-Roussillon Blanc, Palais des Anciens, Vignerons Catalans, Languedoc-Roussillon, France, £7.99, Tesco, 12% (page 70)
- 2010 Cuvée Pêcheur, Vin de France, £4.35, Waitrose, 11.5% (page 98)
- 2010 Cuvée de Richard, Comté Tolosan, South-West France, £4.99, Majestic, 11.5%
- 2010 Côtes du Rhône Blanc, César, Dom. Roche-Audran, Rhône Valley, France, £15, Christopher Piper, 12%
- 2010 VdP du Gers, Lesc, Producteurs Plaimont, South-West France, £5.65, Caves de Pyrène, 11.5%
- 2010 VdP du Gers, Pujalet, South-West France, £4.99, Waitrose, 11.5%
- 2010 Falanghina, Beneventano, Campania, Italy, £5.99, 12% (page 86)
- 2010 Gavi, la Battistina, Araldica, Piedmont, Italy, £7.95, The Wine Society, 12%
- 2009 Gringet, Vin de Savoie, Le Feu, Dom. Belluard, France, £14.52, Caves de Pyrène, 12%
- 2010 Grüner Veltliner, Federspiel, Weissenkirchen, Domäne Wachau, Wachau, Austria, £9.99, Majestic, 12%
- 2010 Grüner Veltliner (Höpler), Austria, £6.99, Tesco Finest, 12%
- 2010 Grüner Veltliner (Markus Huber), Niederösterreich, Austria, £7.99, Sainsbury's TTD, 12%
- 2009 Grüner Veltliner, Terraces, Domäne Wachau, Wachau, Austria, £9.99, Waitrose, 12% (page 57)
- 2010 Iglesia Vella, Dom. du Roc des Anges, Languedoc-Roussillon, France, £28.99, Caves de Pyrène, 12%
- 2010 Muscadet Côtes de Grandlieu sur lie, Fief Guérin, Loire Valley, France, £6.99, Waitrose, 12%
- 2010 Muscadet Sèvre et Maine sur lie, Loire Valley, France, £6.49, Sainsbury's TTD, 12%
- 2009 Muscadet Sèvre et Maine sur lie, Vieilles Vignes, Clos des Allées, Pierre Luneau-Papin, Loire Valley, France, £9.72, Caves de Pyrène, 12%
- 2010 Ortega-Reichensteiner-Chardonnay English White, (Denbies), England, £8.79, Tesco Finest, 12%

- 2009 Petit Chablis, Dom. d'Elise, Burgundy, France, £11.25, Stone, Vine & Sun, 12% (page 64)
- 2009 Petit Chablis, Dom. Gérard Tremblay, Burgundy, France, £10.50, Caves de Pyrène, 12%
- Pinot Grigio, Matra Mountain, Hungary, £5.99, Waitrose, 12% (page 87)
- 2010 Pinot Grigio, Villa Malizia, IGT Venezie, Italy, £3.99, Aldi, 12% (page 99)
- 2010 Riesling, Tim Adams, Clare Valley, South Australia, £10.29, AustralianWineCentre.co.uk, Tesco, 11.5% (page 28)
- 2008 Riesling, Asda Extra Special (Knappstein), Clare Valley, South Australia, £8.68, Asda, 12% (page 68)
- 2008 Riesling, Bishops Head, Waipara Valley, New Zealand, £11.33, Private Cellar, 12%
- 2009 Riesling, Select, Framingham, Marlborough, New Zealand, £13.29, Caves de Pyrène, 8.5%
- 2009 Riesling, Main Divide, Pegasus Bay, Waipara, New Zealand, £12.49, Majestic, 11.5% (page 58)
- 2005 Riesling, The Shortlist, McGuigan, Eden Valley, South Australia, £14.99, Majestic, 12%
- 2009 Riesling, Tingleup Vineyards Great Southern, Western Australia, £9.29, Tesco Finest, 11%
- 2010 Riesling, Dr Wagner, Mosel, Germany, £8.99, Waitrose, 8.5%
- 2009 Riesling Kabinett, Ayler Kupp, Weingut Weber, Mosel, Germany, £8.99, Majestic, 8%
- 2009 Riesling Kabinett, Oberhäuser Leistenberg, Dönnhoff, Nahe, Germany, £16.95, Caves de Pyrène, 9%
- 2009 Riesling Kabinett, Piesporter Goldtröpfchen, Hain, Mosel, Germany, £12.30, Tanners, 8% (page 60)
- 2008 Riesling Kabinett Trocken, Prinz von Hessen, Rheingau, Germany, £9.99, Majestic, 11.5%
- 2010 Riesling Kabinett, Ürziger Würzgarten, Dr Loosen, Mosel, Germany, c.£7, Waitrose, 7.5% (page 58)
- 2010 Rioja Blanco, Valdepomares, Spain, £5.99, M&S, 12% (page 87)
- 2010 Sauvignon Blanc, Bella, Invivo, Marlborough, New Zealand, £14, Harvey Nichols, 9%
- 2010 Sauvignon Blanc, Champteloup, Touraine, Loire Valley, France, £7.79, Waitrose, 12%
- 2010 Sauvignon Blanc, La Grille, Touraine, Loire Valley, France, £6.99, Majestic, 12%
- 2010 Sauvignon Blanc, Les Rafelières, Vin de Pays du Val de Loire, Sauvion, France, £8.27, Private Cellar, 12%
- 2010 Sauvignon Blanc, Touraine (Pierre Chainier), Loire Valley, France, £7.99, Sainsbury's TTD, 12%
- 2010 Savagnin, Springhill, Irvine, Eden Valley, South Australia, £14.25, Vin du Van, 12% (page 60)
- 2010 Semillon, Tim Adams, Clare Valley, South Australia, £11.25, AustralianWineCentre.co.uk, Tesco, 12% (page 33)
- 2010 Semillon, Denman Vineyard, Hunter Valley, New South Wales, Australia, £9.99, Tesco Finest, 11%
- 2005 Semillon, Mount Pleasant Elizabeth, Hunter Valley, New South Wales, Australia, £11.99, Tesco, Wine Rack, 12% (page 39)
- 2006 Semillon (McWilliam's/Sainsbury's TTD), Hunter Valley, New South Wales, Australia, £8.99, 10.5% (page 47)
- 2010 Semillon-Chardonnay, Peter Lehmann, Barossa, South Australia, £8.99, Sainsbury's, 11.5%
- 2010 Soave Classico (Equipe), Veneto, Italy, £4.29, Tesco, 12% (page 99)
- 2010 Soave, Vignale, Veneto, Italy, £4.99, Waitrose, 12% (page 89)
- 2009 Viña Esmeralda, Torres, Catalunya, Spain, c.£7.50, widely available, 11.5%

- 2010 Viña Sol, Torres, Catalunya, Spain, c.£7, widely available, 11.5%
- 2010 Vinho Verde Branco, Loureiro, Afros, Portugal, £10.20, Caves de Pyrène, 12%
- 2010 Vinho Verde, Quinta de Azevedo, Sogrape, Portugal, c.£7.40, Majestic, Waitrose, 11.5% (page 72)

Rosé wine

- 2010 Cuvée Fleur, Vin de France, £4.35, Waitrose, 12%
- 2010 English Rosé, Chapel Down, £9.99, Waitrose, 11%
- NV Grenache Rosé, Plume, Dom. la Colombette, VdP Coteaux du Libron, Languedoc-Roussillon, France, £6.29, Booths, 9% (page 107)
- 2010 Pinot Noir Rosé, Fairleigh Estate, Marlborough, New Zealand, £7.49, Majestic, 11%
- 2010 Pinot Rosé, Pays d'Oc, Dom. Begude, Languedoc, France, £8.99, Majestic, 11.5%
- 2010 Rosé d'Anjou, Champteloup, Loire Valley, France, £6.99, Waitrose, 11%
- 2010 Txacoli Rosado, Ameztoi, País Vasco, Spain, £10.50, Caves de Pyrène, 10.5%
- 2010 Utiel-Requena, Toro Loco Rosé, Valencia, Spain, £3.49, Aldi, 12%

Red wine

- 2010 Bergerie de la Bastide, Vin de Pays d'Oc, Languedoc-Roussillon, France, £5.29, Caves de Pyrène, 12%
- 2010 Bourgueil, Trinch!, C & P Breton, Loire Valley, France, £11.95, Caves de Pyrène, 12%
- 2010 Cheverny, Clos du Tue-Boeuf, Loire Valley, France, £10.89, Caves de Pyrène, 11.5%
- 2010 Côte Roannaise, Dom. Robert Sérol, Loire Valley, France, £9.75, Christopher Piper, 12%
- 2010 Cuvée Chasseur, Vin de France, £4.35, Waitrose, 12%
- 2010 Cuvée de Richard, Pays d'Aude, Languedoc-Roussillon, France, £4.99, Majestic, 12%
- 2010 Gamay, VdP de l'Ardèche, Rhône Valley, France, £4.49, Marks & Spencer, 12%
- 2008 Gamay, La Mule, Vin de France, Dom. Chahut & Prodiges, Loire Valley, France, £12.15, Caves de Pyrène, 12%
- 2010 Gamay, Henry Marionnet, Touraine, Loire Valley, France, £9.55, Caves de Pyrène, 12%
- 2010 Gamay, Mon Cher, Noëlla Morentin, Loire Valley, France, £13.69, Caves de Pyrène, 12%
- 2010 Marzemino delle Venezie, Italy, £5.99, Sainsbury's TTD, 12%
- 2009 Mauvais Temps, VdP de l'Aveyron, Dom. Nicolas Carmarens, South-West France, £15.30, Caves de Pyrène, 11.5%
- 2010 Negroamaro del Salento, La Casada Caleo, Puglia, Italy, £6.49, Caves de Pyrène, 12%
- 2010 Reggiano Rosso, Emilia-Romagna, Italy, £5.99, M&S, 12%
- 2010 Syrah, VdP de l'Ardèche, Dom. Romaneaux-Destezet/Souhaut, Rhône Valley, France, £17.76, Caves de Pyrène, 11.5%
- 2010 Trinacria Rosso, Sicily, Italy, £3.99, Waitrose, 12%
- NV Valpolicella (House), Veneto, Italy, £4.49, Sainsbury's, 11.5%
- 2010 Valpolicella, Vignale, Veneto, Italy, £4.99, Waitrose, 12%
- 2010 Valpolicella, Villa Molino, Italy, £6.49, M&S Wine Direct, 12%

FIZZ

After a time of recession, I would have hoped that this year's Champagnes would be of better quality, as producers clamoured to attract their customers back with more exciting wines. But it hasn't really happened like that. A few of the top branded Champagnes have come out guns blazing – Charles Heidsieck, Pol Roger and Bollinger to name three – but many of the big labels are producing unambitious, bland wines and charging us mightily for the privilege of being disappointed by them. So you won't be finding them in this guide. Instead you'll find a bunch of wines that make you feel good at reasonable prices. Most of the Champagnes are over £20 because that's how the world is. If you don't like the price, well, there are some pretty good own-label Champagnes, or you must move away from Champagne. The success of English fizz – Coates & Seely, Gusbourne, Jenkyn Place and Meopham Valley are exciting new wines this year – and Prosecco shows that people are increasingly prepared to drink the alternative with no sense that they're dumbing down. They're not. It's a tough world out there. Drink whatever you like at the price that suits you. There's nothing more likely to make you feel ill at ease and unhappy than knowing you've paid more than you can afford just because you thought you had to. You don't.

• The wines are listed in descending price order.

2004 Champagne Brut, Premier Cru, Pierre Vaudon (Union Champagne), France, 12.5% abv
Haynes, Hanson & Clark, £30.60

Pierre Vaudon does an immensely reliable non-vintage cuvée that always has enough maturity to pass as something more expensive, but this is the single-harvest vintage wine. 2004 is a relatively quick-maturing vintage – and this matches youthful freshness with maturity, brightness with depth, drinkability with ageability. Drink it now for its fresh cream, hint of savoury nut and splash of chocolate syrup, but it will age for 5–10 years if you want all the flavours to get more powerful and impressive.

2004 Champagne Brut, Premier Cru, De Saint Gall (Union Champagne), France, 12.5% abv
M&S, £30

M&S get this from my favourite creator and blender of big volumes of fizz, Union Champagne at Avize, where they have access to some of the best Chardonnay grapes in all of Champagne – and they put them to good effect here. This is a 100% Chardonnay wine with all the lovely, soft, biscuity, yeasty style this king of white grapes gives. Nutty too, creamy even, this is top stuff now, but will age.

2006 Classic Cuvée, Nyetimber, West Sussex, England, 12% abv
Waitrose, Averys, D Byrne, Oxford Wine Co, other independents, £29.99

It was Nyetimber who started the whole idea of English fizz being able to take on – and beat – the world. In those early days – the 1990s – the wines were high in acid but aged on their yeast lees for so long that they became amazingly biscuity and rich. Nyetimber is now in the throes of developing a more crowd-friendly style. 2006 is a sort of halfway house. There's some very ripe, almost raisined, fruit in there as well as the traditional deep flavours of loft apples, months old but still good to eat, and some syrupy yeasty roundness to soothe the customary Nyetimber acidity.

2006 English Sparkling Wine, Blanc de Blancs, Gusbourne, Kent, England, 12% abv
Armit, £29.99, Halifax Wine Co, £24.50, Noel Young, £25.99

One by one new stars are rising in the English fizz firmament. I first heard the buzz about Gusbourne when people started whispering about a stellar Pinot Noir they'd tasted. But this is fizz, and 100% Chardonnay, a hugely classy effort, easily matching Champagnes of a similar price, though developing a uniquely southern English character and style. It smells of blackcurrant leaves, ripe green apple, rosehip and summer hedgerows. Its acidity is fresh and tingling, not rasping, apple peel and boiled lemons, its richness is of rice pudding cream and hazelnuts, and it will only get deeper and more fascinating if you age it a few years.
• Gusbourne Brut Reserve (c. £25) is equally inspiring.

NV The Society's Champagne Brut, Private Cuvée, Alfred Gratien, France, 12.5% abv
The Wine Society, £26

I'm often asked who my favourite Champagne producer is, and if I had to average out the last 20 years, I might well put the small but perfectly formed house of Alfred Gratien at the top. They don't make much, but they've had a long-standing agreement to make a special blend for the Wine Society, and year by year it delivers triumphantly. This is still young – you can age Alfred Gratien non-vintage for 5–10 years – but it has loads of class and character. The wine positively foams and has a warm, full flavour of baked Bramley apples wrapped in a richness of flaky butter croissants, crème fraîche and nut syrup. That may sound sweet, but it isn't, and it's all tied tightly together by the acidity of Bramley skins and twisted lemon zest.

NV Champagne Brut, Blanc de Noirs, Henri Chauvet, France, 12% abv
Private Cellar, £25.45

Made solely from black grapes, grown in the important village of Rilly. If such wine were simply made into fizz and then sold off young, it would be too raw and unforgiving. But these guys blend about a third of the volume of old wine in with the newer stuff and the result is a revelation. It tastes of several shades of milk chocolate, including a couple of chocolate wafers, and has an unmistakable savoury yeasty quality with more than a hint of Marmite. So you should now know whether you're going to love this or hate it.

• Private Cellar are rather good at these interesting, flavoursome Champagne styles and they have another one you might like, too: Tradition by Legras & Haas (£26).

PRODUCT OF FRANCE

CHAMPAGNE

de BRUYNE

CUVÉE ABSOLUE

BRUT ROSÉ

NV Champagne de Bruyne, Cuvée Absolue Brut Rosé, France, 12% abv
Goedhuis & Co, £24.50

The rather attractive, retiring salmon pink colour warns you that this is not nightclub Champagne – it's too sophisticated for all that malarkey, and it's drier and more mature than the kind of party pop you pay through the nose for at these hangouts. Its dry restraint is a delight. And there's a lot of flavour: nuts and brioche, bready, slightly creamy, but with an attractive savoury overtone, and a flash of apple peel acidity to sharpen it – and you – up.

NV Champagne Brut, Premier Cru (Union Champagne), France, 12.5% abv
Tesco Finest, £19.99

Amazingly reliable wine, considering that Tesco sells a shedload of the stuff. But it does help that they go to the best co-operative cellar in Champagne to make this blend: Union Champagne in the high-quality village of Avize, which successfully supplies several British retailers. Tesco's version is soft, reasonably appley and fresh, with an underlying richness rather like Cornish clotted cream.

- Of the other own-label Champagnes in the supermarkets, Morrisons' is also pretty good (£17.79), supplied by the quality-conscious Champagne house of Boizel.

NV Champagne Brut, Blanc de Noirs (Alexandre Bonnet), France, 12% abv
Waitrose, £18.99

Waitrose used to be famous for their Blanc de Blancs Champagne, from 100% white (Chardonnay) grapes. They then changed suppliers and haven't been able to recapture the magic, so the mantle of excellence has shifted to their Blanc de Noirs – using 100% black (Pinot Noir) grapes. The result is a really good, almost unnervingly full-bodied fizz – but that's the style: black grapes make heavier wine. Ripe apple fruit is enlivened here by a little strawberry scent, and this is round, full and assertive. If you want to drink Champagne with a meal, look no further.

NV Pelorus, Cloudy Bay, Marlborough, New Zealand, 12.5% abv
Majestic, £16.99, Waitrose, £19.49

Exceptional quality: layer upon layer of confectioner's cream and hazelnut, a little crème fraîche yeastiness and full, ripe but dry fruit, all subtly streaked through with acid. Outperforms almost all Champagne at this price. Come to think of it, the winery is owned by the Veuve Clicquot bunch, and I reckon Pelorus outperforms the much pricier Veuve Clicquot Champagne most days.

- Majestic also has 2006 Pelorus (£19.99) and Pelorus Rosé (£16.99).

NV Champagne Brut, Les Pionniers (P & C Heidsieck), France, 12% abv
The Co-operative Group, £17.99

This is made by what is quite possibly the best team in Champagne, the guys at P & C Heidsieck. It's serious wine and would actually benefit from a bit more age. Any of you planning a big celebration next year – buy this now. Unusually for Heidsieck it's made almost entirely from black Pinot grapes, and this gives the wine a broader, more serious structure – less fun and games and dancing in the fountains. But there's fruit here, and creamy depth too, and the firm acidity will soften as the months go by.

NV Primo Secco, Primo Estate, South Australia, 11.5% abv
AustralianWineCentre.co.uk, £14

New from one of Australia's winemaking greats – and as usual with Joe Grilli of Primo Estate, it overdelivers. It's only 11.5% alcohol but it bursts with fresh ripe flavours – apple blossom and blackcurrant leaf aromas, ripe apple flesh fruit and the gentle acid reminder of boiled lemons, all transformed into happy juice by a cascade of soft-edged foam.

NV Crémant de Bourgogne Brut Rosé, Blason de Bourgogne, Burgundy, France, 12% abv
Waitrose, £12.99

Crémant de Bourgogne is a good wine style for those of you wanting to approximate the Champagne experience but at a lower price. This is balanced, quite full-bodied though lean, just hinting at strawberry and cream, but coming down more on the side of chalky austerity.

NV Cienna Rosso, Brown Brothers, Victoria, Australia, 7.5% abv
Waitrose, £9.99

Brown Brothers have always championed new grape varieties. Even so, I don't think I'd have come up with sweet, low-alcohol cherry-purple fizz as my first idea for a new grape variety based on Cabernet Sauvignon! But with loads of cherry and sweet plum, apple peel acidity and oceans of carpet-staining foam, it's bright, playful, flirtatious party fizz.

NV Sparkling Sauvignon Blanc, Lindauer, New Zealand, 12% abv Waitrose, £9.99

This is rather a good idea: full-on, zingy, tangy Kiwi Sauvignon – with bubbles in it. Lindauer already makes good Champagne-like fizz, so soaking up spare Sauvignon for bubbly seemed like a good idea. They simply inject the wine with carbon dioxide, add a bit of truly Champagne-method fizzy Chardonnay to fatten it up, and here it is: gooseberry, blackcurrant leaf, green apples and some pebbly earth – with bubbles in it.

• Virgin Wines also do a good version: Kiki Sparkling
  Sauvignon Blanc (£11.99).

2009 Vintage Cava, Chardonnay, Blanc de Blancs, Single Estate, San Cugat (Freixenet), Spain, 12.5% abv M&S, £9.99

Cava has been displaced as the fun fizz by Prosecco and pushed towards the basement of 'bargain bubbly for a party and not much more'. This is a pity, because there's some pretty good Cava around right now – but it isn't as much 'fun' as Prosecco, and it still needs a real chilling down to hide some of its rougher edges. This one is made from Chardonnay – which is a good start – and foams brightly through a creamy, yeasty flavour speckled with honey and apple spice and rapped by quite firm acidity. And it could age for a year.

- Marques de Montoya at Sainsbury's (£10.99) is also a good soft Cava. At the cheap end, Asda's NV Cava Brut (£4.49) isn't bad, nor is Tesco's NV Cava Brut (£4.49). If you want your Cava pink, go for Morrison's NV Cava Rosado (£6.79) or Asda's NV Cava Rosado (£4.49).

NV Prosecco Brut, San Leo, Italy, 11% abv
Waitrose, £8.99

Italian wines are back in fashion in a big way, and if you're wondering what those cool Italians drink when they want bubbles – Prosecco, that's what. Prosecco has in large part taken over from Cava as the fun fizz – more expensive, but more fun. Prosecco scores in its bright, breezy fruitiness. This one has an easygoing, frothy personality, is reasonably dry and has a good dollop of pear and banana fruit, with, crucially, some apple peel and lemon zest acidity. Without acidity, it would taste blowsy and flat.

- There are several other good Proseccos around. Best of the rest is Prosecco La Marca at Majestic (£9.99). Morrisons Best Prosecco (£9.99) is pretty good, as is Sainsbury's Taste the Difference Prosecco (£10.49). And Morrisons also do a full-flavoured cherry pink fizzy Pinot Grigio Raboso (£9.99).

2010 Moscato d'Asti, Sourgal, Elio Perrone, Piedmont, Italy, 5% abv
The Wine Society, £6.75

Lovely stuff – bursting with fresh fruit flavours, foaming with goodwill and good humour – and only 5% alcohol. The crucial thing with Moscato d'Asti is freshness – so always buy the most recent vintage. This froths on your tongue and hurls flavours of pear juice, boiled lemons, juicy green Muscat grapes, honey, icing sugar and summer dust to all corners of your mouth, with a zingy acid that makes it extra-appetizing. Serve as cold as you like – and if you can't think what to serve with Christmas pudding, try this.

NV Asti Dolce (Araldica), Piedmont, Italy, 7% abv Sainsbury's, £5.13

Delightful stuff. Low in alcohol, high in fruit and fun. Uncomplicated, marvellously grapy — crunchy green Muscat grapes, draped in the musky scent of vines in a hothouse, drizzled with honey and icing sugar and shot through with a lively leafy acidity.

RED FIZZ

NV Sparkling Red (disgorged 2010), Joseph, Primo Estate, South Australia, 13.5% abv
AustralianWineCentre.co.uk, £30

Here it is. The modern history of Australian red wine in a single bottle. There's Shiraz from every vintage since the 1980s, a random selection of early 1960s and 70s Australian red wines, all piled in with a big barrel of Moda Cabernet-Merlot (see page 31) to make the mother of all base wines. It is then liqueured up with old Australian fortified wines — so much age, so much history, so many good and bad times, wines fatigued, wines supernaturally bright. This shouldn't fizz, it shouldn't foam; most of these flavours should be slumbering in the cobwebbed gloom of a forgotten cellar, tasting of leather aprons and smoke and the sweaty sparks of the blacksmith's forge. They shouldn't be in a fresh, young bottle, and, dammit, they shouldn't foam, it's not respectful. This mixes old Burgundian decay, old toffee-prune Shiraz, the withered cream of old Grenache and Mataro, the distant memory of blackberry and blackcurrant when the wines were young and hopeful. All thrown together in this last-chance cauldron, this writhing, foaming medley of old and very old, renewed to laughter and delight by the magic of bubbles.

FORTIFIED WINES

Sherry is going through a period of rediscovery, a confidence-boosting realization that its brilliant traditions and the legion of different flavours the old methods can create are the future as well as the past. Rich, sweet port, on the other hand, seems to be getting caught in a rut. Two companies supply almost all the widely available port in our market, and whereas they used to provide wines of considerably different styles, under various labels, I'm finding too many of them just tasting like 'strong sweet red', a style the Americans are keen on, which are merely variations on – you guessed it – the strong-ness, the sweet-ness and the red-ness of the wine, without much else to differentiate them. Prices are pretty high, too. So I've chosen enough ports to give you some idea of what to buy, but I've spent more time on the sherries, whose prices are amazingly reasonable, and whose flavours are some of the most original in the world. And they don't just rely on strength and sweetness – most of them are bone dry.

- In this section you will find sherries first, then ports, in descending price order.

SHERRY

Manzanilla San León, Bodegas Argüeso, Spain, 15% abv
Waitrose, £10.99

You want dry sherry? It doesn't come much drier than this. Manzanilla is the palest and, often, the most delicate of sherries, but don't come here for delicacy. Come here for a shocking, brilliant haughtiness, an almost arrogant disregard for dumbing down and smoothing out. This has a high cheek-boned serenity that you'll love or hate, a dryness like old banisters, like house dust settling on ancient floorboards scrubbed clean a thousand times; the fruit is like a pale unripe apple peering nervously into watery sunlight, and whatever softness it has is that of bread dough before it's baked. Don't ask me why, but it reminded me of the Bates Motel in *Psycho*. The banisters, perhaps.

Dry Amontillado Sherry, Aged 12 years, Emilio Lustau, Spain, 19% abv
Sainsbury's Taste the Difference, £7.99/50 cl

The classic flavour of dry amontillado is buttered brazil toffees. This doesn't quite catch the buttered brazils, but it is a very good, almost dry yet beautifully rich amber brown sherry. It has a delicious richness of toffee and flapjacks, prunes and roasted nuts and a depth like dark brown sugar – but without the sweetness. Indeed, there's an attractively bitter edge, but the softness and richness hold it back from being austere.

Dry Oloroso Sherry, Aged 12 years, Emilio Lustau, Spain, 20% abv
Sainsbury's Taste the Difference, £7.99/50 cl

Warming, soothing, but properly dry sherry the colour of polished horse chestnuts. It has a beautiful array of old brown flavours – raisins and dried figs, prunes and stewed plums, but they are all dry, wrapped in some kind of sugarless glycerine, and there's an appetizing bitterness nagging at the back of your palate, but it's a bitterness wearing velvet gloves.

Amontillado Maribel, Sánchez Romate, Spain, 19% abv The Wine Society, £7.95

The quality of their sherries alone would be an excellent reason to join the Wine Society. They regularly ship tiny amounts of thrilling old sherries virtually drawn by hand from the barrels by their buying team. Last Christmas I tasted two simply stunning 40-year-old sherries they had discovered – they only bottled 240 half bottles: such wine had never been sold before, it will never be sold again, but they'll find something else just as good. This brilliant Amontillado is their regular stuff. It's as classic an example as you'll find anywhere – and it's less than £8 a bottle. A gorgeous 'childhood memories' smell of buttered brazil caramels, the scent of old leather, dried-out figs and prunes, the ground dust of hazelnut shells and a strange, brilliant, bitter-edged syrupiness that has had all the sweetness sucked out of it by a Dyson Airblade.

Dry Old Palo Cortado, Emilio Lustau, Spain, 19% abv
M&S, £7.49/37.5 cl

This is a very rare style of sherry, so I'm delighted to find it in the High Street, and even more delighted that it's in such good nick. It's such a fascinating wine that you could contemplatively drink the whole bottle yourself and still be coming up with new flavours as you drained the last drop. First things first; this beautiful limpid, amber wine is rigidly, unapologetically dry. Yet it's amazingly smooth and a whole cavalcade of flavours pass over your tongue – do you remember the strange sweet smell of brown manila envelopes? That's there. Dried dates and figs, dried meats, hard nutty cheese – and nuts, yes, hazelnuts, but also a sensation as though you could taste the autumnal shine of the nutshell itself. Dundee cake jousts with orange zest, dusty sultana skins, a hint of Harrogate toffee richness, specks of dust dislodged from an old rectory stairwell. The rest? You'll have to buy a bottle and make it up for yourself.

Dry Old Oloroso, Emilio Lustau, Spain, 20% abv
M&S, £7.49/37.5 cl

Lovely shiny chestnut colour, but with a slight greenness at the rim – a sign that they've used some classy old sherries in this blend. That's what takes this wine past the flavour of figs and raisins and into another exciting but shadowy world of nutty hard cheese, spiced chutney, manila brown envelopes and bitter black chocolate sprinkled with the dust from the bottom of a jar of nuts. Trenchant, I called it (yes, you may well ask), and then I noticed a strange age-withered scent trailing across my palate, searching for the wine I had swallowed.

Manzanilla (Bodegas Williams & Humbert), Spain, 15% abv
M&S, £6.99

Manzanilla is a delicate style of sherry that should really be drunk within three or four months of being bottled. This means the producers should draw off a new batch for bottling from the vats three or four times a year. So I was very encouraged when tasting this wine at M&S that they were so focused on keeping it fresh. My sample had been bottled six weeks previously and would run another couple of months before a new bottling hit the shelves. This is a very good example of the style: bone dry, with a touch of softly sour yeast creaminess, bread crust aroma and a nice, nippy apple peel acidity.

The Society's Fino, Sánchez Romate, Spain, 15% abv
The Wine Society, £5.95

An excellent example of the Wine Society's sherry – and simply outstanding value for money. Fino sherry is bone dry, but a little fuller than manzanilla, a little fatter, even, but it still has that marvellous tangy dryness which makes it such a good appetizer, that almost slightly sour green apple peel acidity and the strange soft-sourness of yeasty bread dough – rather like a malty mixed grain bread in the making. There's also a taste of roasted almonds – and roasted almonds would be the perfect accompaniment.

Manzanilla, Special Reserve (Bodegas Barbadillo), Spain, 15% abv
Tesco Finest, £5.29/50 cl

This is relatively soft – perhaps a little too soft for purists – but it's got that lovely savoury, bready quality that is at the heart of so much good dry sherry. A gentle creaminess, a little walnut flesh, and the kind of water and flour dough I used to make into dampers as a boy scout – a very good, mild introduction to the joys of manzanilla.

• In the same range Tesco has an Amontillado Special Reserve (£5.29), which is bone dry but full of exciting brown flavours like wizened prunes and plums and burnt jam on the edge of an apricot jam tart with the appetizing bitter nip of a hazelnut husk.

MADEIRA

Full Rich Madeira, Henriques & Henriques, Portugal, 19% abv
Connolly's, Oxford Wine Company, Villeneuve, Waitrose, Wright Wine Co, c. £11.99

Henriques & Henriques make fantastic Madeiras, often from single grape varieties. Waitrose sells several of them: they're expensive but well worth it for the unique experience. This is more an introductory style, made from Madeira's all-purpose grape variety, Tinta Negra Mole, but it's brilliant stuff and shows how fantastically different Madeira is from any other wine in the world. It's impressively rich, but it also has a lightning fork of acidity that gorgeously knits all the lush flavours together –

flavours of dates and raisins, but also coffee creams and hazelnut whirl milk chocolate and the scent of clean old leather.

PORT

1994 Vintage Port (Symington Family Estates), Portugal, 20% abv
Tesco Finest, £20.59

This is quite a bargain. 1994 is a helluva year for port – classic, long-lasting stuff. And the Symington Family, who make this, produce some of port's most famous names, such as Warre's, Graham's and Dow's. So you've got loads of pedigree yet are saving a stash of money because the wine is sailing under the Tesco banner. Swallow your pride: this is 17-year-old wine for a little over £20. And it's big, ripe, full of sweet blackberry and rich black cherry fruit with good peppery bite and a satisfying sense of power that tells you you could age it for another 10 years if you wanted to.

10-year old Tawny Port, Taylor's, Portugal, 20% abv
Widely available, c. £20

I feel as though tawny ports have been getting thicker, more liquorous in recent years, losing a lot of the refreshing elegance that used to make them such delightful drinks. This has definitely got the full, brown, interesting flavours that make good tawnies attractive – dried figs, prunes, a little muscovado sugar and some caramelized roasted parsnips. It's also got a touch of sweet-sourness and wood bark bitterness to balance it. The flavours are all there. I'd just like it a little less rich.

Crusted Port (bottled 2003), Graham's, Portugal, 20% abv
Morrisons, Sainsbury's, £16.98

Year by year Graham's Crusted is one of the best high-quality ports you can buy – at a fair price. Crusted is a kind of 'semi-vintage' style, not quite as dense or long-lived as vintage, but offering real perfume and intriguing fruit and spice in a more subdued way. This has a calm quality, unlike the thunderous character of many full-blown vintage wines, its fruit is gentle but sweet, blackberry and blackcurrant nicely balanced by fresh acidity and delightfully scented with orchard blossom, orange zest and a mid-climb suggestion of Kendal mint cake.

2005 Late Bottled Vintage Port (unfiltered, bottled 2010), Fonseca, Portugal, 20% abv
Bibendum, Butlers Wine Cellar, Majestic, £14.99

This is what a good LBV should taste like. There's something not quite right with a lot of the LBVs on the High Street just now; hopefully it's just a phase, but most of them are decidedly short on personality. Luckily, this one's got buckets of it, piled up with sweet blackberries and black plum skins, the rasp of herbs, the bite of peppercorn and an attractive grainy tannic bitterness to go with the syrupy richness. It's good now, but you could age it for 5–10 years.

Pink Port, Portugal, 19.5% abv
M&S, £5.99/50 cl

The invention of pink port has been a breath of fresh air through the fusty halls of port-dom. Several of the supermarkets have Croft Pink Port (Co-op, Morrisons, Sainsbury's, about £10.72) and it's good, but the M&S own-label is brighter, breezier and more fun – garish day-glo candy-floss pink colour, rose petal and red plum scent, and an easy party-going flavour full of cherries and plums and pear flesh, with just a snap of pepper and a waxy softness to keep it pleasurable and unchallenging.

SWEETIES

Sweet wines don't seem to be greatly loved right now. A few merchants still specialize in them and continue to trumpet their merits, but I often wonder whether they retire from their soapboxes to drown the silence of our indifference in a glass or two of the lush golden delights they have such difficulty in persuading us to buy. Is it because times are tough right now that we don't feel it's quite right to drink something so unashamedly indulgent as a sybaritic sticky? But look at it another way. Times are tough. We need to cheer ourselves up. Fine sweet wine is uplifting stuff, and a lot of it is available in half bottles – and therefore at half the price. And if it's just a hefty slug of something sweet to get you through a winter evening that you're after, Moscatel de Valencia's been doing the job for years – at about £3.99 a bottle – and it's not stopped yet.

- The wines are listed in descending price order.
- Many sweet wines are sold in half bottles (37.5 cl) or 50 cl bottles.

2006 St. Laurent, Roter Eiswein, Hölzler, Weinrieder, Niederösterreich, Austria, 12.5% abv
Waterloo Wine Company, £20.55/37.5 cl

This isn't exactly red, but it's certainly not golden or white, either. In fact, the St. Laurent is a red grape, which explains the fatigued orange-pink colour, but it isn't usually made into a sweet wine. This is actually pretty syrupy. It's attractively mature, mixing dense and quite acid apple and plum syrup with something more gooey and treacly – a gold/red fruit of some kind with a hint of the scented bitterness of sloes.

2007 Chaume, Château Soucherie, Loire Valley, France, 13% abv
Fingal-Rock, £19.95

I don't go to Fingal-Rock for the easy option. Their wines are always uncompromising, unadorned with fol-de-rols and chemists' cologne, unfettered by the desire to please. This wine harks back to an age-old sweetness, now soured by experience. There's nothing fresh and brisk about this – it's all antimacassars and eight-course breakfasts – but it has a glorious dowager's hauteur, the volatile sweet sourness of unpicked orchards in late autumn, the fruit neglected apricots and goldengage, the honey powerful but bruised and smeared on apricot and orange shortbread sprinkled with sweet vineyard dust. And long after you've swallowed, a tingling, wistful, sour-sweet aftertaste remains.

1995 Vin Santo del Chianti Rufina, Villa di Monte (Fattoria di Vetrice), Tuscany, Italy, 17% abv
M&S, £15.99/37.5 cl

This is not one of the most monumental of Vin Santos – those are very rare and outrageously expensive – but it'll give you a good idea of the style and would be delicious for dipping with those little cantucci almond biscuits. It's deep and rich rather than massively sweet, but there's a good whack of cherry and fudge and some powerful nutty syrup tinged with a slight dry sherry sourness. A bitter nip at the end makes it a good, contemplative kind of wine.

2010 Rivesaltes Hors d'Age, Reflexió, Castell Pesillà, Languedoc-Roussillon, France, 16% abv
Christopher Piper Wines, £15.77/50 cl

Fabulous example of an ancient sweet wine style from right down near the Pyrenees. Hors d'Age means 'beyond age' – i.e. on the old side – and it is the years of patient maturing that has created these remarkable flavours, caught between autumn sweetness, mineral rasp and citrus peel bitterness. Buttered brazil caramel, old figs and dried apricots rolled in beeswax flood over a minerality as bright and glistening as the washings from a gold prospector's pan; burnt treacle tart and orange zest bitterness keep trying to intrude without ever quite managing it.

2010 La Beryl Blanc, Fairview, Paarl, South Africa, 14% abv
sawinesonline.co.uk, £14.29/50 cl

It's not many wine producers who pick their grapes and then wilfully set out to lose 75% of their liquid – ie their wine – and then name the wine after their mother. But that's what Charles Back does, laying out his best white grapes on straw

mats so that they shrivel in the sun. And I have to say, he makes a helluva wine out of them. Wonderfully warm and waxy, proud, demanding almost, with its insistent acidity continually challenging the sweetness of baked apple tart, pear sponge, apricots with the yeasty sourness of the sponge uncooked, syrup like braided golden hair.

2009 Late Harvest Chardonnay, Waipara West, Waipara, New Zealand, 11% abv

Waterloo Wine Company, £12.80 (£7.80/37.5 cl)

Sweet wines made out of Chardonnay are pretty rare, but it doesn't surprise me to see Waipara West giving it a go – they're already one of New Zealand's more original wine producers. It's unusual, I'll admit, but it works. It's rich, full of quince jelly and goldengage fruit, sweet stewed golden plum skins and loft apples gone shrivelled and dry, flecked with a drop or two of honest toiler's sweat.

NV Muscat Museum Reserve, Yalumba, Victoria, Australia, 18% abv

Flagship Wines, £12.55, Morrisons, £11.99/37.5cl

The great midwinter warmer. These luscious, gooey brown wines from the warm heart of Australia are some

of Down Under's most unsung wonders. Sometimes they are thrillingly aromatic, heavy-lidded with rose petal perfume and the aroma of Darjeeling tea leaves. This one is more concerned with the lush intensity of the superripe juice oozing from the dark-skinned Muscat grapes, dense as treacle tart, dense as brown muscovado sugar dissolved in black syrup, thick with the richness of dates and dried figs and sultanas. It'd be great with ice cream, or *on* ice cream, for that matter.

2009 Brachetto d'Acqui, Cavallino, Il Cascinone, Piedmont, Italy, 5% abv
Harvey Nichols, £10.75, Virgin Wines, £10.99

There's the merest suggestion of foam on this, but not really enough to classify it as fizz. But if you chill this down, it's delightful stuff, bubbles or no bubbles. What other wine offers you a waft of rose petal scent, then a riotous mix of red cherry and strawberry, mouth-watering nectarine flesh, streaked with oranges and marmalade peel. Come to think of it, how good would that be with a slightly livelier bubble?

2007 Botrytis Semillon, Éclat, Valdivieso, Curico Valley, Chile, 9% abv
Bibendum, £8.50/37.5 cl

They don't make a big thing of sweet wines in Chile, but this is a very fair stab at emulating France's great classic sweet wine, Sauternes. They're using the same Semillon grape and have come up with a rich, waxy wine full of peach and apricot sweet fruit, syrup flecked with slightly salty, savoury yeast and orange peel bitterness and a pleasant touch of sweet cake dough.

NV Moscatel Oro, Floralis, Torres, Spain, 15% abv
Majestic, Morrisons, Waitrose, £7.99/50 cl

Torres is best known for dry table wines – red, pink and white – and as anyone who has gone on holiday in Spain knows, they're everywhere, they seem to follow you around, bar to bar, restaurant to restaurant. This is a newer venture – sweet Muscat – and it's got a very attractive, slightly floral perfume that sets you up for a soft, fresh wine, full of the sweet juiciness of the Muscat grape mingling with crystallized honey, dates and a twist of orange peel.

NV Moscatel de Valencia, Cherubino Valsangiacomo, Valencia, Spain, 15% abv
Tesco, £3.99

Ronseal wine. It does what it says on the tin – and doesn't cost you much, either. A whole bundle of sweet flavours: icing sugar and meringue, orange juice, sugared almonds and cheap pink Turkish delight – all soused in satisfyingly chubby syrup.

Storing, serving and tasting

Wine is all about enjoyment, so don't let anyone make you anxious about opening, serving, tasting and storing it. Here are some tips to help you enjoy your wine all the more.

The corkscrew

The first step in tasting any wine is to extract the cork. Look for a corkscrew with an open spiral and a comfortable handle. The Screwpull brand is far and away the best, with a high-quality open spiral. 'Waiter's friend' corkscrews – the type you see used in restaurants – are good too, once you get the knack.

Corkscrews with a solid core that looks like a giant woodscrew tend to mash up delicate corks or get stuck in tough ones. And try to avoid those 'butterfly' corkscrews with the twin lever arms and a bottle opener on the end; they tend to leave cork crumbs floating in the wine.

Corks

Don't be a cork snob. The only requirements for the seal on a bottle of wine are that it should be hygienic, airtight, long-lasting and removable. Real cork is environmentally friendly, but is prone to shrinkage and infection, which can taint the wine. Synthetic closures modelled on the traditional cork are common in budget wines, but the largest increase has been in the use of screwcaps, or Stelvin closures, which are now appearing on some very classy wines, especially in Australia and New Zealand, South Africa and South America.

Decanting

Transferring wine to a decanter brings it into contact with oxygen, which can open up the flavours. You don't need to do this ages before serving and you don't need a special decanter: a glass jug is just as good. And there's no reason why you shouldn't decant the wine to aerate it, then pour it back into its bottle to serve it. Some tough young wines can be transformed by this treatment, and red wines under screwcap also benefit from this.

Mature red wine is likely to contain sediment and needs careful handling. Stand the bottle upright for a day or two to let the sediment fall to the bottom. Open the wine carefully, and place a torch or candle beside the decanter. As you pour, stand so that you can see the light shining through the neck of the bottle. Pour the wine into the decanter in one steady motion and stop when you see the sediment reaching the neck of the bottle.

Temperature

The temperature of wine has a bearing on its flavour. Heavy reds are happy at room temperature, but that phrase 'room temperature' was coined before central heating: 17–19°C/63–66°F is probably the max. The lighter the wine, the cooler it should be. I'd serve Burgundy and other Pinot Noir reds at cool larder temperature. Juicy, fruity young reds, such as wines from the Loire Valley, are refreshing served lightly chilled.

Chilling white wines makes them taste fresher, but also subdues flavours, so bear this in mind if you're splashing out on a top-quality white – don't keep it in the fridge too long. Sparkling wines, however, should be well chilled to avoid exploding corks and fountains of foam.

For quick chilling, fill a bucket with ice and cold water, plus a few spoonfuls of salt if you're in a real hurry. This is much more effective than ice on its own. If the wine is already cool, a vacuum-walled cooler will maintain the temperature.

The wine glass

The ideal wine glass is a fairly large tulip shape, made of fine, clear glass, with a slender stem. This shape helps to concentrate the aromas of the wine and to show off its colours and texture. For sparkling wine choose a tall, slender glass, as it helps the bubbles to last longer.

Look after your glasses carefully. Detergent residues or grease can affect the flavour of any wine and reduce the bubbliness of sparkling wine. Ideally, wash glasses in very hot water and don't use detergent at all. Rinse glasses thoroughly and allow them to air-dry. Store wine glasses upright to avoid trapping stale odours.

Keeping opened bottles

Exposure to oxygen causes wine to deteriorate, but most modern wines may actually improve after being open for a day. If you keep the opened bottle in the fridge, many wines can be delicious after 1–2 weeks. Recorking – or rescrewing the screw cap – is usually enough protection, but you can also buy perfectly effective devices to keep oxygen at bay if you want.

Laying down wine

The longer you intend to keep wine before you drink it, the more important it is to store it with care. If you haven't got a cellar, find a nook – under the stairs, a built-in cupboard or a disused fireplace – that is cool, relatively dark and vibration-free, in which you can store the bottles on their sides to keep the corks moist (if a cork dries out it will let air in and spoil the wine).

Wine should be kept cool – around 10–15°C/50–59°F. It is also important to avoid sudden temperature changes or extremes: a windowless garage or outhouse may be cool in summer but may freeze in winter. Exposure to light can ruin wine, but dark bottles go some way to protecting it from light.

How to taste wine

If you just knock your wine back like a cold beer, you'll be missing most of whatever flavour it has to offer. Take a bit of time to pay attention to what you're tasting and I guarantee you'll enjoy the wine more.

Read the label

There's no law that says you have to make life hard for yourself when tasting wine. So have a look at what you're drinking and read the notes on the back label if there is one. The label will tell you the vintage, the region and/or the grape variety, the producer and the alcohol level.

Look at the wine

Pour the wine into a glass so it is a third full and tilt it against a white background so you can enjoy the range of colours in the wine. Is it dark or light? Is it viscous or watery? As you gain experience, the look of the wine will tell you one or two things about the age and the likely flavour and weight of the wine. As a wine ages, whites lose their springtime greenness and gather deeper, golden hues, whereas red wines trade the purple of youth for a paler brick red.

Swirl and sniff

Give the glass a vigorous swirl to wake up the aromas in the wine, stick your nose in and inhale gently. This is where you'll be hit by the amazing range of smells a wine can produce. Interpret them in any way that means something to you personally: it's only by reacting honestly to the taste and smell of a wine that you can build up a memory bank of flavours against which to judge future wines.

Take a sip

At last! It's time to drink the wine. So take a decent-sized slurp – enough to fill your mouth about a third full. The tongue can detect only very basic flavour elements: sweetness at the tip, acidity at the sides and bitterness at the back. The real business of tasting goes on in a cavity at the back of the mouth that is really part of the nose. The idea is to get the fumes from the wine to rise up into this nasal cavity. Note the toughness, acidity and sweetness of the wine, then suck some air through the wine to help the flavours on their way. Gently 'chew' the wine and let it coat your tongue, teeth, cheeks and gums. Jot down a few notes as you form your opinion and then make the final decision … Do you like it or don't you?

Swallow or spit it out

If you are tasting a lot of wines, you will have to spit as you go if you want to remain upright and retain your judgement. Otherwise, go ahead and swallow and enjoy the lovely aftertaste of the wine.

Wine faults

If you order wine in a restaurant and you find one of these faults, you are entitled to a replacement. Many retailers will also replace a faulty bottle if you return it the day after you open it, with your receipt. Sometimes faults affect random bottles, others may ruin a whole case of wine.

- Cork taint – a horrible musty, mouldy smell indicates 'corked' wine, caused by a contaminated cork.
- Volatile acidity – pronounced vinegary or acetone smells.
- Oxidation – sherry-like smells are not appropriate in red and white wines.
- Hydrogen sulphide – 'rotten eggs' smell.

Watchpoints

- Sediment in red wines makes for a gritty, woody mouthful. To avoid this, either decant the wine or simply pour it gently, leaving the last few centilitres of wine in the bottle.
- White crystals, or tartrates, on the cork or at the bottom of bottles of white wine are both harmless and flavourless.
- Sticky bottle neck – if wine has seeped past the cork it probably hasn't been very well kept and air might have got in. This may mean oxidized wine.
- Excess sulphur dioxide is sometimes noticeable as a smell of a recently struck match; it should dissipate after a few minutes.

Wine style guide

When faced with a shelf – or a screen – packed with wines from around the world, where do you start? Well, if you're after a particular flavour, my guide to wine styles will point you in the right direction.

White wines

Bone-dry, neutral whites

Neutral wines exist for the sake of seafood or to avoid interrupting you while you're eating. It's a question of balance, rather than aromas and flavours, but there will be a bit of lemon, yeast and a mineral thrill in a good Muscadet *sur lie* or a proper Chablis. Loads of Italian whites do the same thing, but Italy is increasingly picking up on the global shift towards fruit flavours and maybe some oak. Basic, cheap South African whites are often a good bet if you want something thirst-quenching and easy to drink. Colombard and Chenin are fairly neutral grape varieties widely used in South Africa, often producing appley flavours, and better examples add a lick of honey.

- Muscadet
- Chenin Blanc and Colombard – from the Loire Valley, South-West France, Australia, California or South Africa
- Basic white Bordeaux and Entre-Deux-Mers
- Chablis
- Pinot Grigio

Green, tangy whites

For nerve-tingling refreshment, Sauvignon Blanc is the classic grape, full of fresh grass, gooseberry and nettle flavours. I always used to go for New Zealand versions, but I'm now equally inclined to reach for a bottle from new-wave producers in Chile, South Africa or Hungary. Or even a simple white Bordeaux –

Bordeaux Sauvignon is buzzing with life. Loire Valley Sauvignons can be overrated, but Touraine can be excellent. Austria's Grüner Veltliner has a peppery freshness. From north-west Spain, Galicia's Albariño grape has a stony, mineral lemon zest sharpness; the same grape is used in Portugal, for Vinho Verde. Alternatively, look at Riesling: Australia serves it up with aggressive lime and mineral flavours; New Zealand and Chile give milder versions of the same style. Alsace Riesling is lemony and dry, while German Rieslings go from bone-dry to intensely sweet, with the tangiest and zestiest coming from the Mosel Valley.

- Sauvignon Blanc – from New Zealand, Chile, Hungary, South Africa, or Bordeaux
- Loire Valley Sauvignons, especially Touraine, but also Sancerre and Pouilly-Fumé
- Riesling – from Australia, Austria, Chile, Germany, New Zealand, or Alsace in France
- Grüner Veltliner from Austria
- Vinho Verde from Portugal and Albariño from north-west Spain

Intense, nutty whites

The best white Burgundy from the Côte d'Or cannot be bettered for its combination of soft nut and oatmeal flavours, subtle, buttery oak and firm, dry structure. Prices are often hair-raising, but cheaper wines from single producers can offer a glimpse of real Burgundy style. For around £8–10 your best bet is oaked Chardonnay from an innovative Spanish region such as Somontano, or around Limoux in South-West France. You'll get a nutty, creamy taste and nectarine fruit with good oak-aged white Bordeaux or traditional white Rioja. Top Chardonnays from New World countries – and Italy for that matter – can emulate Burgundy, but we're looking at serious prices.

- White Burgundy – including Meursault, Pouilly-Fuissé, Chassagne-Montrachet, Puligny-Montrachet
- White Bordeaux – including Pessac-Léognan, Graves
- White Rioja
- Chardonnay from New Zealand and Oregon – and top examples from California and Australia (Western Australia and Victoria)

Ripe, toasty whites

Aussie Chardonnay conquered the world with its upfront flavours of peaches, apricots and melons, usually spiced up by the vanilla, toast and butterscotch richness of new oak. This winning style has now become a standard-issue flavour produced by all sorts of countries, rarely to any great effect. You'll need to spend a bit more than a fiver nowadays if you want something to relish beyond the first glass. Oaked Australian Semillon can also give rich, ripe fruit flavours, as can oaked Chenin Blanc from South Africa. If you see the words 'unoaked' or 'cool-climate' on an Aussie bottle, expect an altogether leaner drink.

- Chardonnay: from Australia, Chile, California, South Africa, Spain
- Oak-aged Chenin Blanc from South Africa
- Australian Semillon

Aromatic whites

Alsace has always been a plentiful source of perfumed, dry or off-dry whites: Gewurztraminer with its rose and lychee scent or Muscat with its floral, hothouse grape perfume. A few producers in New Zealand, Australia, Chile and South Africa are having some success with these grapes. Floral, apricotty Viognier, traditionally the grape of Condrieu in the northern Rhône, now appears in vins de pays from all over southern France and also from California and Australia. Condrieu is expensive (£20 will get you entry-level stuff and no guarantee that it will be fragrant); vin de pays/IGP wines start at around £5 and can be good. For aroma on a budget, grab some Hungarian Irsai Olivér or Argentinian Torrontés. English white wines often have a fresh, floral hedgerow scent – the Bacchus grape is one of the leaders of this style.

- Alsace whites, especially Gewurztraminer and Muscat
- Gewürztraminer from Austria, Chile, Germany, New Zealand and cooler regions of Australia
- Condrieu, from the Rhône Valley in France
- Viognier from southern France, Argentina, Australia, California, Chile
- English white wines, especially Bacchus
- Irsai Olivér and Cserszegi Füszeres from Hungary
- Torrontés from Argentina

Golden, sweet whites

Good sweet wines are difficult to make and therefore expensive: prices for Sauternes and Barsac (from Bordeaux) can go through the roof, but near-neighbours Monbazillac, Loupiac, Saussignac and Ste-Croix-du-Mont are more affordable. Sweet Loire wines such as Quarts de Chaume, Bonnezeaux and some Vouvrays have a quince aroma and a fresh acidity that can keep them lively for decades, as do sweet Rieslings such as Alsace Vendange Tardive, German and Austrian Beerenauslese (BA), Trockenbeeren-auslese (TBA) and Eiswein. Canadian icewine is quite rare over here, but we're seeing more of Hungary's Tokaji, with its sweet-sour, marmalade flavours.

- Sauternes, Barsac, Loupiac, Sainte-Croix-du-Mont
- Monbazillac, Saussignac, Jurançon and Pacherenc du Vic-Bilh from South-West France
- Loire sweet whites such as Bonnezeaux, Quarts de Chaume and Vouvray moelleux
- Auslese, Beerenauslese and Trockenbeerenauslese from Germany and Austria
- Eiswein from Germany, icewine from Canada
- Botrytis Semillon, Riesling or Gewürztraminer from Australia, New Zealand and South Africa

Red wines
Juicy, fruity reds

The definitive modern style for easy-going reds. Tasty, refreshing and delicious with or without food, they pack in loads of crunchy fruit while minimizing the tough, gum-drying tannins that characterize most traditional red wine styles. Beaujolais (made from the Gamay grape) is the prototype – and if you're distinctly underwhelmed by the very mention of the word 'Beaujolais', remember that the delightfully named Fleurie, St-Amour and Chiroubles also come from the Beaujolais region. Loire reds such as Chinon and Saumur (made from Cabernet Franc) pack in the fresh raspberries. Italy's Bardolino is light and refreshing, as is young Valpolicella. Nowadays, hi-tech producers all over the world are working the magic with a whole host of grape varieties. Carmenère, Malbec and Merlot are always good bets, and

Grenache/Garnacha and Tempranillo usually come up with the goods. Italian grapes like Bonarda, Barbera and Sangiovese seem to double in succulence under Argentina's blazing sun. And at around £6–7 even Cabernet Sauvignon – if it's from somewhere warm like Australia, South America, South Africa or Spain – or a vin de pays Syrah from southern France, will emphasize the fruit and hold back on the tannin.

- Beaujolais – including Brouilly, Chiroubles, Fleurie, Juliénas, Moulin-à-Vent, St-Amour. Also wines made from the Gamay grape in other parts of France
- Loire reds: Chinon, Saumur, Saumur-Champigny – and, if you're lucky, Bourgueil, Cheverny and St-Nicolas-de-Bourgueil
- Grenache (from France) and Garnacha (from Spain)
- Carmenère from Chile
- Basic Merlot from just about anywhere
- Inexpensive Argentinian reds, especially Bonarda, but also Sangiovese and Tempranillo

Silky, strawberryish reds

Here we're looking for some special qualities, specifically a gorgeously smooth texture and a heavenly fragrance of strawberries, raspberries or cherries. We're looking for soft, decadent, seductive wines.

One grape – Pinot Noir – and one region – Burgundy – stand out, but prices are high to astronomical. Good red Burgundy is addictively hedonistic and all sorts of strange decaying aromas start to hover around the strawberries as the wine ages. Pinot Noirs from New Zealand, California, Oregon and cool parts of Australia such as Mornington Peninsula, Tasmania and Yarra Valley come close, but they're expensive, too; Chilean Pinots are far more affordable. You can get that strawberry perfume (though not the silky texture) from other grapes in Spain's Navarra, Rioja and up-coming regions like La Mancha and Aragón. Southern Rhône blends can deliver if you look for fairly light examples of Côtes du Rhône-Villages or Costières de Nîmes.

- Red Burgundy – including Chassagne-Montrachet, Beaune, Nuits-St-Georges, Pommard, Givry
- Pinot Noir from Australia, California, Chile, New Zealand, Oregon
- Spanish reds from Rioja, Navarra, La Mancha and Valdepeñas, especially with Tempranillo as the main grape
- Red blends from the southern Rhône Valley, such as Costières de Nîmes, Côtes du Rhône-Villages
- Australian Grenache

Intense, blackcurranty reds

Firm, intense wines that often only reveal their softer side with a bit of age; Cabernet Sauvignon is the grape, on its own or blended with Merlot or other varieties. Bordeaux is the classic region, and with global warming more and more producers can achieve this style, but some wines, especially from villages in the Haut-Médoc, need a few years to develop to a heavenly cassis and cedar maturity. Areas like St-Émilion and Pomerol will achieve this flavour more quickly. The rest of the world has moved to a riper, fruitier style. Chile does the fruity style par excellence. New Zealand can deliver Bordeaux-like flavours, but in a faster-maturing wine. Australia sometimes adds a medicinal eucalyptus twist, but can overripen the fruit to something approaching jam. Argentina and South Africa are making their mark too. In Spain, Ribera del Duero can also come up with blackcurrant flavours, if the wines are not too ripe.

- Bordeaux reds such as Côtes de Castillon, St-Émilion, Pomerol, Moulis, Margaux
- Cabernet Sauvignon from just about anywhere
- Cabernet Sauvignon-Merlot blends

Spicy, warm-hearted reds

Australian Shiraz is the epitome of this rumbustious, riproaring style: dense, rich, chocolaty, sometimes with a twist of pepper, a whiff of smoke, or a slap of leather. But it's not alone. There are southern Italy's Primitivo and Nero d'Avola, California's Zinfandel, Mexico's Petite Sirah, Argentina's Malbec, South Africa's Pinotage, Toro from Spain and some magnificent Greek reds. In southern France the wines of the Languedoc often show this kind of warmth, roughed up with hillside herbs. And if you want your spice more serious, more smoky and minerally, go for the classic wines of the northern Rhône Valley.

- Australian Shiraz, as well as blends of Shiraz with Grenache and Mourvèdre/Mataro – and Durif
- Northern Rhône Syrah (Cornas, Côte-Rôtie, Hermitage, St-Joseph) and southern Rhône blends such as Châteauneuf-du-Pape and Gigondas
- Southern French reds, such as Corbières, Coteaux du Languedoc, Côtes du Roussillon, Faugères, Fitou, Minervois
- Italian reds such as Primitivo, Aglianico, Negroamaro and Nero d'Avola
- Zinfandel and Petite Sirah reds
- Argentinian Malbec
- South African Pinotage

Mouthwatering, sweet-sour reds

Sounds weird? This style is primarily the preserve of Italy, and it's all about food: the rasp of sourness cuts through rich, meaty food, with a lip-smacking tingle that works equally well with pizza or tomato-based pasta dishes. But there's fruit in there too – cherries and plums – plus raisiny sweetness and a herby bite. The wines are now better made than ever, with more seductive fruit, but holding on to those fascinating flavours. All sorts of native Italian grape varieties deliver this delicious sour-cherries taste: Sangiovese (the classic red grape of Tuscany), Nebbiolo (from Piedmont), Barbera, Dolcetto, Teroldego, Sagrantino… You'll have to shell out at least a tenner for decent Chianti, more for Piedmont wines (especially Barolo and Barbaresco, so try Langhe instead). Valpolicella can be very good, but choose with care. Portugal reveals something of the same character in its reds.

- Chianti, plus other wines made from the Sangiovese grape
- Barolo, Barbaresco and other wines made from the Nebbiolo grape
- Valpolicella Classico, Amarone della Valpolicella
- Southern Italian reds
- Alentejo, Tejo and other Portuguese reds

Delicate (and not-so-delicate) rosé

Dry rosé can be wonderful, with flavours of strawberries and maybe raspberries and rosehips, cherries, apples and herbs, too. Southern France and northern Italy are best for delicate pinks. Grapes like Cabernet, Syrah or Merlot give more flavour, or go for Grenache/Garnacha or Tempranillo from the Rhône Valley and Spain. South America is a good bet for flavoursome, fruit-forward pink wine. *See pages 103–7 for my top pinks this year.*

Drink organic – or even biodynamic

- The widely discussed benefits of organic farming – respect for the environment, minimal chemical residues in our food and drink – apply to grapes as much as to any other produce. Full-blown organic viticulture forbids the use of synthetic fertilizers, herbicides or fungicides; instead, cover crops and companion planting encourage biodiversity and natural predators to keep the soil and vines healthy. Warm, dry climates like the South of France, Chile and South Africa have the advantage of rarely suffering from the damp that can cause rot, mildew and other problems – we should be seeing more organic wines from these regions. Organic wines from European countries are often labelled 'Biologique', or simply 'Bio'.
- Biodynamic viticulture takes working with nature one stage further: work in the vineyard is planned in accordance with the movements of the planets, moon, sun and cosmic forces to achieve health and balance in the soil and in the vine. Vines are treated with infusions of mineral, animal and plant materials, applied in homeopathic quantities, with some astonishing results.
- If you want to know more, the best companies to contact are Vinceremos and Vintage Roots (see Retailers' Directory).

Sparkling wines

Champagne can be the finest sparkling wine on the planet, but fizz made by the traditional Champagne method in Australia, New Zealand or California – often using the same grape varieties – is often just as good and cheaper. It might be a little more fruity, where Champagne concentrates on bready, yeasty or nutty aromas, but a few are dead ringers for the classic style. Fizz is also made in other parts of France: Crémant de Bourgogne is one of the best. England is now beginning to rival Champagne in style. Italy's Prosecco is soft and delicately scented. Spain's Cava is available at bargain basement prices in all the big supermarkets, but pay a bit more and you'll get a much better wine.

• Champagne
• Traditional method fizz made from Chardonnay, Pinot Noir and Pinot Meunier grapes grown in Australia, California, England, New Zealand, South Africa
• Crémant de Bourgogne, Crémant de Loire, Crémant de Jura, Crémant d'Alsace, Blanquette de Limoux
• Cava
• Prosecco
• Sekt is Germany's sparkling wine, and is occasionally 100 per cent Riesling
• Lambrusco from Italy is gently sparkling and usually red
• Sparkling Shiraz – an Aussie speciality – will make a splash at a wild party

Fortified wines

Tangy, appetizing fortified wines

To set your taste buds tingling, fino and manzanilla sherries are pale, perfumed, bone dry and bracingly tangy. True amontillado, dark and nutty, is also dry. Dry oloroso adds deep, raisiny flavours. Palo cortado falls between amontillado and oloroso; manzanilla pasada is an older, nuttier manzanilla. The driest style of Madeira, Sercial, is steely and smoky; Verdelho Madeira is a bit fuller and richer, but still tangy and dry.

- Manzanilla and fino sherry
- Dry amontillado, palo cortado and dry oloroso sherry
- Sercial and Verdelho Madeira

Rich, warming fortified wines

Raisins and brown sugar, dried figs and caramelized nuts – do you like the sound of that? Port is the classic dark sweet wine, and it comes in several styles, from basic ruby, to tawny, matured in cask for 10 years or more, to vintage, which matures to mellowness in the bottle. The Portuguese island of Madeira produces fortified wines with rich brown smoky flavours and a startling bite of acidity: the sweet styles to look for are Bual and Malmsey. Decent sweet sherries are rare; oloroso dulce is a style with stunningly concentrated flavours; PX is like treacle. In southern France, Banyuls and Maury are deeply fruity fortified wines. Marsala, from Sicily, has rich brown sugar flavours with a refreshing sliver of acidity. The versatile Muscat grape makes luscious golden wines all around the Mediterranean, but also pops up in orange, black, and the gloriously rich, treacly brown versions that Australia does superbly.

- Port
- Bual and Malmsey Madeira
- Marsala
- Rich, sweet sherry styles include Pedro Ximénez, oloroso dulce
- Vins doux naturels from southern France: Banyuls, Maury
- Fortified (liqueur) Muscat 'stickies' from Australia

Buying wine for the long term

Most of this book is about wines to drink more or less immediately – that's how modern wines are made, and that's what you'll find in most high street and online retail outlets. If you're looking for a mature vintage of a great wine that's ready to drink – or are prepared to wait 10 years or more for a great vintage to reach its peak – specialist wine merchants will be able to help; the internet's another good place to look for mature wines. Here's my beginners' guide to buying wine for drinking over the longer term.

Auctions

A wine sale catalogue from one of the UK's auction houses will have wine enthusiasts drooling over names they certainly don't see every day. Better still, the lots are often of mature vintages that are ready to drink. Before you go, find out all you can about the producer and vintages described in the catalogue. My annually updated *Pocket Wine Book* is a good place to start, or *Michael Broadbent's Vintage Wines* for old and rare wines; *Decanter*, the national wine magazine, runs regular features on wine regions and their vintages. You can also learn a lot from tutored tastings – especially 'vertical' tastings, which compare different vintages. This is important, because some merchants take the opportunity to clear inferior vintages at auction.

The drawbacks? You have no guarantee that the wine has been well stored, and if it's faulty you have little chance of redress. As prices of the most sought-after wines have soared, so it has become profitable either to forge the bottles and their contents or to try to pass off stock that is clearly out of condition. But for expensive and mature wines, I have to say that the top auction houses make a considerable effort to check the provenance and integrity of the wines. Don't forget that there will usually be a commission or buyers' premium to pay, so check out the small print in the sale catalogue. Online wine auctions have similar pros and cons.

If you've never bought wine at an auction before, a good place to start would be a local auctioneer such as Straker Chadwick in Abergavenny (tel: 01873 852624, www.strakerchadwick.co.uk) or Morphets in Harrogate (tel: 01423 530030, www.morphets.co.uk); they're less intimidating than the famous London houses of Christie's and Sotheby's and you may come away with some really exciting wine.

Buying en primeur

En primeur is a French term for wine that is sold before it is bottled, sometimes referred to as a 'future'. In the spring after the vintage, the Bordeaux châteaux – and a few other wine-producing regions, particularly Burgundy and the Rhône in good vintages – hold tastings of barrel samples for members of the international wine trade. The châteaux then offer a proportion of their production to the wine merchants (*négociants*) in Bordeaux, who in turn offer it to wine merchants around the world at an opening price.

The advantage to the châteaux is that their capital is not tied up in expensive stock for the next year or two, until the wines are bottled and ready to ship. Traditionally merchants would buy en primeur for stock to be sold later at a higher price, while offering their customers the chance to take advantage of the opening prices as well. The idea of private individuals investing rather than institutions took off with a series of good Bordeaux vintages in the 1980s; it's got ever more hectic since then.

Wine for the future

There is a lot to be said for buying en primeur. For one thing, in a great vintage you may be able to find the finest and rarest wines far more cheaply than they will ever appear again. Every classic vintage in Bordeaux opens at a higher and higher price, but that price never permanently drops, and so the top wines increase in value, whatever price they start at. Equally, when a wine – even a relatively inexpensive one – is made in very limited quantities, buying en primeur may be practically your only chance of getting hold of it.

In the past, British wine merchants and their privileged customers were able to 'buy double what you want, sell half for double what you paid, and drink for free', but as the market has opened up to people more interested in making a quick buck than drinking fine wine, the whole process has become more risky.

Another potential hazard is that a tasting assessment is difficult at an early date. There is a well-founded suspicion that many barrel samples are doctored (legally) to appeal to the most powerful consumer critics, in particular the American Robert Parker and the *Wine Spectator* magazine. The wine that is finally bottled may or may not bear a resemblance to what was tasted in the spring following the vintage. In any case, most serious red wines are in a difficult stage of their evolution in the spring, and with the best will in the world it is possible to get one's evaluation wrong. However, the aforementioned Americans, magazines like *Decanter*, the broadsheet newspapers and various blogs, will do their best to offer you accurate judgements on the newly offered wines, and most merchants who make a primeur offer also write a good assessment of the wines. You will find that many of them quote the Parker or *Wine Spectator* marks. Anything over 95 out of 100 risks being hyped and hiked in price. Many of the best bargains get marks between 85 and 89, since the 90+ marks are generally awarded for power rather than subtlety. Consideration can be given to the producer's reputation for consistency and to the general vintage assessment for the region.

Bordeaux swings and roundabouts

Prices can go down as well as up. They may not increase significantly for some years after the en primeur campaign. Some popular vintages are offered at ridiculously high prices, but it's only about twice a decade that the combination of high quality and fair prices offers the private buyer a chance of a guaranteed profit. Interestingly, if one highly touted vintage is followed by another, the prices for the second one often have to fall because the market simply will not accept two inflated price structures in a row. Recent Bordeaux examples of this are the excellent 2004 after the much-hyped 2003, and the fine 2001 after the understandably hyped 2000. Sadly this message doesn't always get through. Opening prices for 2005 were as much as 400% up on 2004 for the top wines. The less exciting 2006s dropped by a mere 15% from 2005's vastly inflated level. 2009 opened at historically high prices; the equally good 2010 opened even higher.

But the point to remember is that these crazy headline prices are for the top wines. Modern Bordeaux makes more and more good red each year, and the prices rise modestly, if at all. So while top 2005s and 2006s might rise by £1000 a year per case, the vast majority, not overpraised by critics or craved by the affluent new Asian markets, have hardly moved, except for enforced changes due to a weak pound. 2009 and 2010 have both been offered at record prices. But while for a top property that might mean savage increases, for lesser properties, the increase might only be a pound or two a bottle. In which case, do you really need to buy the current vintage en primeur? Not unless you are solely an investor. And even then you'd be better off buying top properties' wines from vintages like 2008 and 2006. These have been moving up in price appreciably, while 2009 and 2010 stagnate. If you want truly classic wine, buy 2005s. They seemed expensive when they were first offered; they now look positively cheap. Their prices will be on the move before long.

Secure cellarage

Another worry is that the merchant you buy the wine from may not still be around to deliver it to you two years later. Buy from a well-established merchant you trust, with a solid trading base in other wines.

Once the wines are shipped you may want your merchant to store the wine for you; there is usually a small charge for this. If your merchant offers cellarage, you should insist that (1) you receive a stock certificate; (2) your wines are stored separately from the merchant's own stocks; and (3) your cases are identifiable as your property. All good merchants offer these safeguards as a minimum service.

Check the small print

Traditional wine merchants may quote prices exclusive of VAT and/or duty: wine may not be the bargain it first appears. A wine quoted en primeur is usually offered on an ex-cellars (EC) basis; the price excludes shipping, duties and taxes such as VAT. A price quoted in bond (IB) in the UK includes shipping, but excludes duties and taxes. Duty paid (DP) prices exclude VAT. You should check beforehand the exact terms of sale with your merchant, who will give you a projection of the final 'duty paid delivered' price.

Retailers' directory

All these retailers have been chosen on the basis of the quality and interest of their lists. If you want to find a local retailer, turn to the Who's Where directory on page 192. Case = 12 bottles

The following services are available where indicated:
C = cellarage   **G** = glass hire/loan   **M** = mail/online order   **T** = tastings and talks

A & B Vintners

Little Tawsden, Spout Lane, Brenchley, Kent TN12 7AS (01892) 724977 fax (01892) 722673
email info@abvintners.co.uk website www.abvintners.co.uk hours Mon–Fri 9–6 cards MasterCard, Visa
delivery 1–4 cases £12 + VAT within M25; £17 Home Counties; free for 5 cases or more within these areas; phone for
information on other areas minimum order 1 mixed case en primeur Burgundy, Languedoc, Rhône. C M T
✪ Specialists in Burgundy, the Rhône and southern France, with a string of top-quality domaines from all three regions.

Adnams

head office & mail order Sole Bay Brewery, Southwold, Suffolk IP18 6JW (01502) 727222 fax (01502) 727223
email customerservices@adnams.co.uk website www.adnams.co.uk hours (Orderline) Mon–Fri 9–5.30
shops • Adnams Wine Shop, Pinkney's Lane, Southwold, Suffolk IP18 6EW Mon–Sat 9.30–5.30, Sun 10–4
• Adnams Cellar & Kitchen Store, 4 Drayman Square, Southwold, Suffolk IP18 6GB Mon–Sat 9–6, Sun 10–4
• Other shops in: Essex (Saffron Walden), Lincolnshire (Stamford), Norfolk (Harleston, Holt, Norwich, Wells-next-the-Sea),
Suffolk (Hadleigh, Woodbridge), Surrey (Richmond-upon-Thames)
cards AmEx, Maestro, MasterCard, Visa, Delta delivery Free for orders over £50 in most of mainland UK, otherwise £7.50
en primeur Bordeaux, Burgundy, Chile, Rhône. G M T
✪ Extensive list of personality-packed wines from around the world, chosen by Adnams' enthusiastic team of buyers.

Aldi Stores

head office Holly Lane, Atherstone CV9 2SQ; over 400 stores in the UK customer service 0844 406 8800
website www.aldi.co.uk hours Mon–Fri 9–8, Sat 8.30–8, Sun 10–4 (selected stores; check website)

cards Maestro, MasterCard, Visa Debit, Solo.

✪ *Decent everyday stuff from around the world, with lots of wines under £4.*

armit

mail order/online 5 Royalty Studios, 105 Lancaster Road, London W11 1QF (020) 7908 0600 fax (020) 7908 0601
email info@armit.co.uk website www.armit.co.uk hours Mon–Fri 8.45–5.15 cards Maestro, MasterCard, Visa
delivery Free over £250, otherwise £15 delivery charge minimum order 1 case
en primeur Bordeaux, Burgundy, Italy, Rhône, New World. C M T

✪ *Top-quality wines from around the world, with a focus on Bordeaux, Burgundy and Italy. Particularly strong on wines to go with food – they supply some of the country's top restaurants.*

ASDA

head office Asda House, Southbank, Great Wilson Street, Leeds LS11 5AD (0113) 243 5435
customer service (0800) 952 0101; 385 stores website www.asda.co.uk
hours Selected stores open 24 hours, see local store for details cards Maestro, MasterCard, Visa.

✪ *Large and generally successful range of good-value wines at all price points, selected by Philippa Carr MW.*

AustralianWineCentre.co.uk

mail order/online PO Box 3854, Datchet, Slough SL3 3EN 0800 756 1141 fax (01753) 208040
email customerservice@AustralianWineCentre.co.uk website www.AustralianWineCentre.co.uk
cards MasterCard, Visa delivery Free for orders over £100, otherwise £5 per order; UK mainland only
minimum order 12 bottles.

✪ *The original Aussie specialist with some brilliant Australian wines.*

Averys Wine Merchants

head office 4 High Street, Nailsea, Bristol BS48 1BT 0843 224 1224 fax (01275) 811101 email enquiries@averys.com
website www.averys.com • Shop and Cellars, 9 Culver Street, Bristol BS1 5LD (0117) 921 4146 fax (0117) 922 6318
email cellars@averys.com hours Mon–Fri 8–8, Sat–Sun 9–6; Shop Mon–Sat 10–7 cards Maestro, MasterCard, Visa
delivery £6.99 per delivery address en primeur Bordeaux, Burgundy, Port, Rhône. C G M T

✪ *A small but very respectable selection from just about everywhere in France, Italy and Spain, as well as some good stuff from New Zealand, Australia and Chile.*

Bancroft Wines

mail order Woolyard, 54 Bermondsey Street, London SE1 3UD (020) 7232 5440 fax (020) 7232 5451
email sales@bancroftwines.com website www.bancroftwines.com hours Mon–Fri 9–5.30 cards Delta, Maestro, MasterCard, Visa discounts Negotiable delivery £15–25 for London and mainland UK; free for 3 cases or more or for orders of £350 or more (5 cases and £500 outside M25) en primeur Bordeaux, Burgundy, Rhône. C M T
✪ *Bancroft are UK agents for an impressive flotilla of French winemakers: Burgundy, Rhône, Loire and southern France. There is also a fantastic selection of Italian, Spanish and New World wines.*

Bat & Bottle

Unit 5, 19 Pillings Road, Oakham LE15 6QF (01572) 759735 email ben@batwine.co.uk website www.batwine.co.uk
hours Mon–Fri 10–4, Sat 9–2; ring or check website before visiting cards Maestro, MasterCard, Visa
delivery Free for orders over £150. G M T
• Ben's Wine Shop, 10 Northgate, Oakham, Rutland LE15 6QS (01572) 759735 hours Fri 10–7.30, Sat 9–2
✪ *Ben and Emma Robson specialize in Italy, and in characterful wines from small producers. They sell a few favourites from elsewhere, too.*

Bennetts Fine Wines

High Street, Chipping Campden, Glos GL55 6AG (01386) 840392 fax (01386) 840974 hours Mon–Sat 9.30–6
• Edward Sheldon, New Street, Shipston-on-Stour, Warwickshire CV36 4EN (01608) 661409 fax (01608) 663166
hours Mon–Wed 9–6, Thur–Fri 9–7, Sat 9.30–6 email shop@bennettsfinewines.com
website www.bennettsfinewines.com cards Access, Maestro, MasterCard, Visa discounts On collected orders of 1 case or more delivery £6 per case, minimum charge £12, free for orders over £200 en primeur Burgundy, California, New Zealand, Rhône. G M T
✪ *Reasonable prices for high-calibre producers – there's lots to choose from at around £10. Mainly from France and Italy, but some good German, Spanish, Portuguese, Australian and New Zealand wines, too.*

Berkmann Wine Cellars

10–12 Brewery Road, London N7 9NH (020) 7609 4711 fax (020) 7607 0018 email orders@berkmann.co.uk
• Brunel Park, Vincients Road, Bumpers Farm, Chippenham, Wiltshire SN14 6NQ (01249) 463501
fax (01249) 463502 email orders.chippenham@berkmann.co.uk
• Churchill Vintners, 401 Walsall Road, Perry Bar, Birmingham B42 1BT (0121) 356 8888
fax (0121) 356 1111 email sales@churchill-vintners.co.uk

• Pagendam Pratt Wine Cellars, 16 Marston Moor Business Park, Rudgate, Tockwith, North Yorkshire YO26 7QF (01423) 357567 fax (01423) 357568 email orders@pagendampratt.co.uk
website www.berkmann.co.uk hours Mon–Fri 9–5.30 cards Maestro, MasterCard, Visa delivery Free for orders over £150 to UK mainland (excluding the Highlands) minimum order 1 mixed case G M T
✪ UK agent for many top wineries around the world. An incredibly diverse list, with some great Italian wines.

Berry Bros. & Rudd

3 St James's Street, London SW1A 1EG 0800 280 2440 hours Mon–Fri 10–6, Sat 10–5
sales and services 0800 280 2440 (lines open Mon–Fri 9–6, Sat 10–4) fax 0800 280 2443
email bbr@bbr.com website www.bbr.com cards AmEx, Diners, Maestro, MasterCard, Visa
delivery Free to most areas of the UK for orders of £100 or more en primeur Bordeaux, Burgundy, Rhône. C G M T
• Berrys' Bin End Shop, Hamilton Close, Houndmills, Basingstoke, Hampshire RG21 6YB 0800 280 2440
hours Mon–Fri 10–6, Sat–Sun 10–4
✪ Classy and wide-ranging list. There's an emphasis on the classic regions of France. Berry's Own Selection is extensive, with wines made by world-class producers.

Bibendum Wine

mail order 113 Regents Park Road, London NW1 8UR (020) 7449 4120 fax (020) 7449 4121
email sales@bibendum-wine.co.uk website www.bibendum-wine.co.uk hours Mon–Fri 9–5.30
cards Maestro, MasterCard, Visa delivery Free throughout mainland UK for orders over £350, otherwise £15
en primeur Bordeaux, Burgundy, New World, Rhône, Port. M T
✪ Equally strong in the Old World and the New: St Cosme in the Rhône and Vietti in Piedmont are matched by d'Arenberg and Katnook from Australia and Catena Zapata from Argentina.

Big Red Wine Company

mail order Barton Coach House, The Street, Barton Mills, Suffolk IP28 6AA (01638) 510803
email sales@bigredwine.co.uk website www.bigredwine.co.uk hours Mon–Sat 9–6 cards AmEx, Delta, Maestro, MasterCard, Visa, PayPal discounts 5–15% for Wine Club members; negotiable for large orders
delivery £7 per consignment for orders under £200, £10 for orders under £50, UK mainland
en primeur Bordeaux, Rhône, South-West France. C G M T
✪ Intelligently chosen, reliably individualistic wines from good estates in France, Italy and Spain. A list worth reading, full of information and provocative opinion – and they're not overcharging.

Booths

central office Longridge Road, Ribbleton, Preston PR2 5BX (01772) 693800; 27 stores across the North of England **fax** (01772) 693893 **website** www.everywine.co.uk, www.booths.co.uk **hours** Office: Mon–Fri 8.30–5; shop hours vary **cards** AmEx, Electron, Maestro, MasterCard, Visa **discounts** 5% off any 6 bottles. **G M T**

✪ *A list for any merchant to be proud of, never mind a supermarket. There's plenty around £5, but if you're prepared to hand over £7–9 you'll find some really interesting stuff.*

Bordeaux Index

mail order/online 10 Hatton Garden, London EC1N 8AH (020) 7269 0700 **fax** (020) 7269 0701 **email** sales@bordeauxindex.com **website** www.bordeauxindex.com **hours** Mon–Fri 8.30–6 **cards** AmEx, Maestro, MasterCard, Visa **delivery** (Private sales only) free for orders over £2000 UK mainland; visit the website for other delivery details, including international **minimum order** £400 **en primeur** Bordeaux, Burgundy, Rhône, Italy. **C M T**

✪ *Extensive list of fine wines, including older vintages, focused on the classic regions of France and Italy, but with interesting stuff from elsewhere.*

Budgens Stores

head office Musgrave House, Widewater Place, Moorhall Road, Harefield, Uxbridge, Middlesex UB9 6NS 0870 050 0158 **fax** 0870 050 0159; 190 stores mainly in southern England and East Anglia – for nearest store call 0800 298 0758 **email** customerservice@musgrave.co.uk **website** www.budgens.co.uk **hours** Variable; usually Mon–Sat 8–8, Sun 10–4 **cards** Maestro, MasterCard, Visa.

✪ *These days you can be reasonably confident of going into Budgens and coming out with something you'd really like to drink.*

The Butlers Wine Cellar

247 Queens Park Road, Brighton BN2 9XJ (01273) 698724 **fax** (01273) 622761 **email** henry@butlers-winecellar.co.uk • 88 St George's Road, Kemptown, Brighton BN2 1EE (01273) 621638 **hours** Tues–Sat 12–8pm **website** www.butlers-winecellar.co.uk **hours** Mon–Wed, Fri 11–7, Thur, Sat 11–8, Sun 12–6 **cards** Access, AmEx, Maestro, MasterCard, Visa **delivery** Free nationally over £150 **en primeur** Bordeaux. **G M T**

✪ *Henry Butler personally chooses the wines and there is some fascinating stuff here, including English wines from local growers such as Breaky Bottom and Ridgeview. Check the website or join the mailing list as offers change regularly.*

The following services are available where indicated: **C** = cellarage **G** = glass hire/loan **M** = mail/online order **T** = tastings and talks

Anthony Byrne Fine Wines

mail order Ramsey Business Park, Stocking Fen Road, Ramsey, Cambs PE26 2UR (01487) 814555
fax (01487) 814962 email anthony@abfw.co.uk or gary@abfw.co.uk website www.abfw.co.uk
hours Mon–Fri 9–5.30 cards MasterCard, Visa discounts Available on cases delivery Free 5 cases or more, or orders
of £250 or more; otherwise £15 minimum order 1 case en primeur Bordeaux, Burgundy, Rhône. C M T
✪ *A serious range of Burgundy; smaller but focused lists from Bordeaux and the Rhône; carefully selected wines from
Alsace, Loire and Provence; and a wide range of New World.*

D Byrne & Co

Victoria Buildings, 12 King Street, Clitheroe, Lancashire BB7 2EP (01200) 423152 website www.dbyrne-finewines.co.uk
hours Mon–Wed, Sat 8.30–6, Thur–Fri 8.30–8 cards Maestro, MasterCard, Visa delivery Free within 40 miles;
nationally £10 1st case, further cases additional £2.50 en primeur Bordeaux, Burgundy, Rhône, Germany. G M T
✪ *A family business since the 1870s and one of northern England's best wine merchants. A hugely impressive range of
wines, as well as over 300 malt whiskies and over 30 vodkas. I urge you to go and see for yourself.*

Cambridge Wine Merchants

head office 29 Dry Drayton Industries, Scotland Road, Dry Drayton CB23 8AT (01954) 214528 fax (01954) 214574
email cambridgewine@cambridgewine.com website www.cambridgewine.com
• 42 Mill Road, Cambridge CB1 2AD (01223) 568993 email mill@cambridgewine.com
• 32 Bridge Street, Cambridge CB2 1UJ (01223) 568989 email bridge@cambridgewine.com
• 2 King's Parade, Cambridge CB2 1SJ (01223) 309309 email kings@cambridgewine.com
• 163 Cherry Hinton Road, Cambridge CB1 7BX (01223) 214548 email cherry@cambridgewine.com
• 12 Church Street, Ampthill MK45 2PL (01525) 405929 email ampthill@cambridgewine.com
• 34b Kneesworth Street, Royston SG8 5AB (01763) 247076 email royston@cambridgewine.com
• 5 Winchester Street, Salisbury SP1 1HB (01722) 324486 email salisbury@cambridgewine.com
• Edinburgh Wine Merchants, 30b Raeburn Place, Edinburgh EH4 IHN (0131) 343 2347
email stockbridge@edinburghwine.com hours Mon–Sat 10am–9pm, Sun 12–8 cards Amex, MasterCard, Switch, Visa
discounts Buy 4 bottles, get the cheapest one free (selected lines) delivery Free for 12 bottles or more within 5 miles of
Cambridge; £2.50 for less than 12 bottles. National delivery £7.50 per case of 12 bottles; £9.99 for 1 to 11 bottles
en primeur Bordeaux, Burgundy, Rhône, Port. C G M T
✪ *Young, unstuffy merchants with a well-chosen list: good, individual producers, with particularly interesting Australian,
German, Champagne and dessert sections. They're also very serious about port. Every branch has a wine tasting club.*

Les Caves de Pyrène

Pew Corner, Old Portsmouth Road, Artington, Guildford GU3 1LP (office) (01483) 538820 (shop) (01483) 554750
fax (01483) 455068 email sales@lescaves.co.uk website www.lescaves.co.uk hours Mon–Fri 9–5
cards Maestro, MasterCard, Visa delivery Free for orders over £180 within London, elsewhere at cost
discounts Negotiable minimum order 1 mixed case en primeur South-West France. G M T
✪ *Excellent operation; devotees of 'natural wines'. France and Italy are particularly strong and there's some choice stuff from Spain, Australia and New Zealand.*

Cockburns of Leith

mail order/online Thistle House, Caputhall Road, Deans Industrial Estate, Livingston EH54 8AS (01506) 468 900
fax (01506) 414 486 email imacphail-cockburns@wine-importers.net website www.cockburnsofleith.co.uk
hours Mon–Fri 9–5 cards Maestro, MasterCard, Visa delivery Free 12 or more bottles within Edinburgh; elsewhere
£9.99 en primeur Bordeaux, Burgundy. M
✪ *Scotland's oldest surviving wine merchant, founded in 1796; under new ownership since 2010. Most major wine regions covered. Older vintages of Bordeaux, Burgundy and the Rhône.*

Connolly's Wine Merchants

Arch 13, 220 Livery Street, Birmingham B3 1EU (0121) 236 9269/3837 fax (0121) 233 2339
website www.connollyswine.co.uk hours Mon–Fri 9–5.30, Sat 10–4 cards AmEx, Maestro, MasterCard, Visa
delivery National delivery available (charges apply) discounts 10% for 12 or more bottles
en primeur Burgundy. G M T
✪ *Award-winning merchant that has something for everyone. Burgundy, Bordeaux and the Rhône all look very good; and there are top names from Germany, Italy, Spain and California. Weekly in-store tastings, monthly tutored tastings and winemaker dinners. Birmingham's largest whisky retailer, too.*

The Co-operative Group

head office New Century House, Manchester M60 4ES Freephone 0800 0686 727 for stock details; approx. 3200 licensed
stores email customer.relations@co-op.co.uk website www.co-operative.coop hours Variable cards Variable.
✪ *Champions of Fairtrade. The Co-op is stocking some good wine at the moment, most of it under £10. A small list of fine wines between £10 and £20 available in premium stores. The Co-operative Group bought the Somerfield chain in 2009.*

Corney & Barrow

head office No. 1 Thomas More Street, London E1W 1YZ (020) 7265 2400 fax (020) 7265 2444 hours Mon–Fri 8–6 (24-hr answering machine) email wine@corneyandbarrow.com website www.corneyandbarrow.com
• Corney & Barrow East Anglia, Belvoir House, High Street, Newmarket CB8 8DH (01638) 600000 hours Mon–Sat 9–6
• Corney & Barrow (Scotland) with Whighams of Ayr, 8 Academy Street, Ayr KA7 1HT (01292) 267000
hours Mon–Sat 10–5.30
• Oxenfoord Castle, by Pathhead, Midlothian EH37 5UD (01875) 321921 hours Mon–Fri 9–6
cards AmEx, Maestro, MasterCard, Visa delivery Free for all orders above £200 within mainland UK, otherwise £12.50
per delivery. en primeur Bordeaux, Burgundy, Champagne, Rhône, Italy, Spain. C G M T
✪ *Top names in French and other European wines; Australia, South Africa and South America are also impressive. Wines in every price bracket – try them out at Corney & Barrow wine bars in London.*

DeFINE Food & Wine

Chester Road, Sandiway, Cheshire CW8 2NH (01606) 882101 fax (01606) 888407
email office@definefoodandwine.com website www.definefoodandwine.com
hours Mon–Sat 10–7, Sun 11–2 cards AmEx, Maestro, MasterCard, Visa
discounts 5% off 12 bottles or more delivery Free locally, otherwise £7.50 UK. C G M T
✪ *Wine shop and delicatessen, with British cheeses and many food specialities from Italy and Spain. Excellent, wide-ranging list of over 1000 wines including a strong line-up from Argentina, New Zealand and South Africa, as well as European classics.*

Devigne Wines

mail order PO Box 13748, North Berwick EH39 9AA (01620) 890860 fax (05600) 756 287
email info@devignewines.co.uk website www.devignewines.co.uk hours Mon–Fri 10–6 cards AmEx, Maestro,
MasterCard, Visa discounts Selected mixed cases at introductory rate delivery Free for orders over £300, otherwise
£6.50 per consignment; please ring for quote for Highlands and islands. M
✪ *Small list specializing in French wine: traditional-method sparkling wines from all over France; a wide choice of rosés; Gaillac from the South-West; and wines from the Languedoc and the Jura.*

Direct Wine See Laithwaites.

The following services are available where indicated: C = cellarage **G** = glass hire/loan **M** = mail/online order **T** = tastings and talks

Direct Wine Shipments

5–7 Corporation Square, Belfast, Northern Ireland BT1 3AJ (028) 9050 8000
fax (028) 9050 8004 email shop@directwine.co.uk and info@directwine.co.uk website www.directwine.co.uk
hours Mon–Fri 9.30–7 (Thur 10–8), Sat 9.30–5.30 cards Delta, Electron, Maestro, MasterCard, Solo, Switch, Visa
discounts 10% in the form of complementary wine with each case delivery Free Northern Ireland 1 case or more, variable
delivery charge for UK mainland depending on customer spend en primeur Bordeaux, Burgundy, Rhône. C M T
✪ *Rhône, Spain, Australia and Burgundy outstanding; Italy, Germany and Chile not far behind; there's good stuff from pretty
much everywhere. Wine courses, tastings and expert advice offered.*

Nick Dobson Wines

mail order 38 Crail Close, Wokingham, Berkshire RG41 2PZ 0800 849 3078 fax 0870 460 2358
email nick.dobson@nickdobsonwines.co.uk website www.nickdobsonwines.co.uk hours Mon–Fri 9–5
cards Access, Maestro, MasterCard, Visa delivery £8.95 + VAT 1 case; £7.95 + VAT 2nd and subsequent cases to UK
mainland addresses. M T
✪ *Specialist in wines from Switzerland, Austria and Beaujolais, plus intriguing selections from elsewhere in Europe and
Israel.*

Domaine Direct

mail order 6–9 Cynthia Street, London N1 9JF (020) 7837 1142 fax (020) 7837 8605
email mail@domainedirect.co.uk website www.domainedirect.co.uk hours Mon–Fri 8.30–6 or answering machine
cards Maestro, MasterCard, Visa delivery Free London; elsewhere in UK mainland 1 case £15.32, 2 cases £21.44,
3 cases £24, 4 or more free and for all orders over £400 + VAT. minimum order 1 mixed case
en primeur Burgundy (in top vintages). C M T
✪ *Sensational Burgundy list; prices are very reasonable for the quality. Also a full range from Western Australia star
Leeuwin Estate.*

Farr Vintners

mail order/online only 220 Queenstown Road, Battersea, London SW8 4LP (020) 7821 2000 fax (020) 7821 2020
email sales@farrvintners.com website www.farrvintners.com hours Mon–Fri 9–6 cards Access, Maestro, MasterCard,
Visa delivery London £1 per case (min £15); elsewhere at cost minimum order £500 + VAT en primeur Bordeaux. C M T
✪ *A fantastic list of the world's finest wines. The majority is Bordeaux, but you'll also find top stuff and older vintages
of white Burgundy, red Rhône, plus Italy, Australia and California.*

Fingal-Rock

64 Monnow Street, Monmouth NP25 3EN tel & fax 01600 712372 email tom@pinotnoir.co.uk
website www.pinotnoir.co.uk hours Mon 9.30–1.30, Thur & Fri 9.30–5.30, Sat 9.30–5 cards Maestro, MasterCard,
Visa discounts 5% for at least 12 bottles collected from shop, 7.5% for collected orders over £500, 10% for collected
orders over £1200 delivery Free locally (within 30 miles); orders further afield free if over £100. G M T
✪ *The website address gives you a clue that the list's great strength is Burgundy, especially reds. There are wines from
some very good growers and at a range of prices between £8 and £40. Small but tempting selections from other French
regions, as well as other parts of Europe and the New World and wines from local producer, Monnow Valley.*

Flagship Wines

417 Hatfield Road, St Albans, Hertfordshire AL4 0XP (01727) 865309 email sales@flagshipwines.co.uk
website www.flagshipwines.co.uk hours Tues–Thur 11–6, Fri 11–7.30, Sat 10–6 cards Maestro, MasterCard, Visa
delivery Free to St Albans addresses and £10 to other UK mainland addresses. G M T
✪ *Independent whose prices can match those of the supermarkets – plus friendly, well-informed advice from boss Julia
Jenkins. Strong in Australia, New Zealand, France and Spain but great stuff all round. Programme of tastings and events.*

Fortnum & Mason

181 Piccadilly, London W1A 1ER (020) 7734 8040 fax (020) 7437 3278 ordering line (020) 7973 4136
email info@fortnumandmason.co.uk website www.fortnumandmason.com hours Mon–Sat 10–8, Sun 12–6 (Food
Hall and Patio Restaurant only) cards AmEx, Diners, Maestro, MasterCard, Visa discounts 1 free bottle per unmixed
dozen delivery £4.95 per delivery address en primeur Bordeaux. M T
✪ *Impressive names from just about everywhere, including Champagne, Bordeaux, Burgundy, Italy, Germany,
Australia, New Zealand, South Africa and California. Impeccably sourced own-label range.*

Friarwood

26 New King's Road, London SW6 4ST (020) 7736 2628 fax (020) 7731 0411
email simon.mckay@friarwood.com; christina@friarwood.com website www.friarwood.com
• 35 West Bowling Green Street, Edinburgh EH6 5NX (0131) 554 4159 fax (0131) 554 6703
email edinburgh@friarwood.com
hours Mon–Sat 10–7 cards AmEx, Diners, Maestro, MasterCard, Visa, Solo, Electron discounts 5% on cases of 12
(mixed and unmixed) delivery (London) Free within M25 and on orders over £200 in mainland UK; (Edinburgh) free locally
and on orders over £200 en primeur Bordeaux. C G M T

❂ *The focus is Bordeaux, including mature wines from a good selection of petits châteaux as well as classed growths. Burgundy and other French regions are strong, too.*

FromVineyardsDirect.com
online only Northburgh House, 10 Northburgh Street, London EC1V 0AT (020) 7549 7900 fax (020) 7253 9539
email info@fromvineyardsdirect.com website www.fromvineyardsdirect.com hours 9.30–6.30 cards Maestro,
MasterCard, Visa, Solo, Switch delivery Free minimum order 1 case (12 bottles) in UK mainland; 2 cases in Northern
Ireland, Scottish Highlands and islands en primeur Bordeaux. C M T
❂ *A hand-picked selection of wines direct from vineyards in France, Italy and Spain, at very affordable prices.*

Gauntleys of Nottingham
4 High Street, Exchange Arcade, Nottingham NG1 2ET (0115) 911 0555 fax (0115) 911 0557
email rhône@gauntleywine.com website www.gauntleys.com hours Mon–Sat 9–5.30 cards Maestro, MasterCard, Visa
delivery 1 case £11.95, 2–3 cases £9.95, 4 or more cases free minimum order 1 case en primeur Alsace, Burgundy,
Loire, Rhône, southern France, Spain. M T
❂ *They've won many awards for their Rhône and Alsace lists. Loire, Burgundy, southern France and Spain are also excellent.*

Goedhuis & Co
6 Rudolf Place, Miles Street, London SW8 1RP (020) 7793 7900 fax (020) 7793 7170 email sales@goedhuis.com
website www.goedhuis.com hours Mon–Fri 9–5.30 cards Maestro, MasterCard, Visa delivery Free on orders over £250
ex-VAT; otherwise £15 ex-VAT England, elsewhere at cost minimum order 1 unmixed case en primeur Bordeaux,
Burgundy, Rhône. C G M T
❂ *Fine wine specialist. Bordeaux, Burgundy and the Rhône are the core of the list, but everything is good. A sprinkling of New World producers, too.*

Great Northern Wine
The Warehouse, Blossomgate, Ripon, North Yorkshire HG4 2AJ (01765) 606767 fax (01765) 609151
email info@greatnorthernwine.co.uk website www.greatnorthernwine.co.uk hours Tues–Wed 9–7, Thur–Sat 9–11
cards Maestro, MasterCard, Visa discounts 10% on case quantities delivery Free locally, elsewhere at cost
en primeur Bordeaux. G M T
❂ *Independent shippers who seek out interesting wines from around the world. There's also a wine bar, where you can enjoy wines bought in the shop (£5 corkage charge).*

Great Western Wine

Wells Road, Bath BA2 3AP (01225) 322810 (enquiries) or (01225) 322820 (orders) fax (01225) 427231
email orders@greatwesternwine.co.uk website www.greatwesternwine.co.uk hours Mon–Fri 10–7, Sat 10–6
cards AmEx, Maestro, MasterCard, Visa discounts 5% off mixed cases, 10% off unsplit cases delivery Free for 12
bottles or more in UK mainland; £8.95 for smaller orders en primeur Australia, Bordeaux, Burgundy, Rioja. C G M T
❂ *Wide-ranging list, bringing in brilliant wines from individual growers around the world. Also organizes events and tastings.*

Peter Green & Co

37A/B Warrender Park Road, Edinburgh EH9 1HJ (0131) 229 5925 email shop@petergreenwines.com
website www.petergreenwines.co.uk hours Tues–Thur 10–6.30, Fri 10–7.30, Sat 10–6.30 cards Maestro, MasterCard,
Visa discounts 5% on unmixed half-dozens delivery Free in Edinburgh minimum order (For delivery) 1 case. G T
❂ *Extensive and adventurous list: Tunisia, India and the Lebanon rub shoulders with the more classic countries.*

Green & Blue

36–38 Lordship Lane, East Dulwich, London SE22 8HJ (020) 8693 9250 email info@greenandbluewines.com
website www.greenandbluewines.com hours Mon–Wed 9–11, Thur–Sat 9–midnight, Sun 11–8
cards Delta, Maestro, MasterCard, Visa discounts 5% off mixed cases of 12 (collection only), 10% on unmixed cases
delivery Free within 2 miles for over £200, otherwise £10 per delivery within M25; £10 per case outside M25. G T
❂ *A tempting list full of unusual wines you really want to drink – and you can try them on the spot, in the friendly wine bar,
which serves tapas-style food. The staff are knowledgeable, and there's a waiting list for the popular tutored tastings.*

Halifax Wine Company

18 Prescott Street, Halifax, West Yorkshire HX1 2LG (01422) 256333 email andy@halifaxwinecompany.com
website www.halifaxwinecompany.com hours Tues–Thur 9–5, Fri 9–6, Sat 9–5. Closed first week in January and first
week in August cards Access, Maestro, MasterCard, Visa discounts 8% on 12 bottles or more (can be unsplit cases) for
personal callers to the shop delivery Free to HX postcodes on orders over £85; rest of UK mainland – delivery charges
apply depending on order value. M
❂ *Exciting, wide-ranging and award-winning list, at keen prices. Portugal (fantastic list of Madeiras), Spain and Italy are the
strong points but there is plenty from the New World, too.*

The following services are available where indicated: C = cellarage G = glass hire/loan M = mail/online order T = tastings and talks

Handford Wines

105 Old Brompton Road, South Kensington, London SW7 3LE (020) 7589 6113 fax (020) 7581 2983
email mick@handford.net website www.handford.net hours Mon–Sat 10–8.30, Sun 11–5
cards AmEx, Maestro, MasterCard, Visa discounts 5% on mixed cases delivery £8.50 for orders under £150 within UK
en primeur Bordeaux, Burgundy, Rhône, Port. G M T
✪ Delightful London shop, absolutely packed with the sort of wines I really want to drink.

hangingditch wine merchants

Britannic Buildings, 42–44 Victoria Street, Manchester M3 1ST (0161) 832 8222
email wine@hangingditch.com website www.hangingditch.com hours Mon–Wed 10–6, Thur–Sat 10–8, Sun 1–5
cards AmEx, MasterCard, Visa, all debit cards discounts 5% on 6–11 bottles, 10% on 12 bottles or more
delivery free for cases within 10 miles; national deliveries: £7.50 for up to 12 bottles G M T
✪ Primarily a wine merchant but also promotes the 'vinoteca' concept – wines by the glass available from a rotating
selection or by the bottle for retail price plus a fixed £6 corkage. Food and wine matching and bespoke tasting events and
gourmet dinners also on offer.

Roger Harris Wines

mail order Loke Farm, Weston Longville, Norfolk NR9 5LG (01603) 880171 fax (01603) 880291
email vikki@rogerharriswines.co.uk website www.rogerharriswines.co.uk hours Mon–Fri 9–5 cards AmEx,
MasterCard, Visa delivery UK mainland, £4 for 1st case, £2 every additional case minimum order 1 mixed case. M
✪ Britain's acknowledged experts in Beaujolais also have a good range of white wines from the neighbouring Mâconnais
region.

Harvey Nichols

109–125 Knightsbridge, London SW1X 7RJ (020) 7201 8537 hours Mon–Sat 10–8, Sun 12–6
• The Mailbox, 31–32 Wharfside Street, Birmingham B1 1RE (0121) 616 6024 hours Mon–Sat 10–7, Sun 11–5
• 30–34 St Andrew Square, Edinburgh EH2 2AD (0131) 524 8322 hours Mon–Wed 10–6, Thur 10-8, Fri, Sat 10–7,
Sun 11–6
• 107–111 Briggate, Leeds LS1 6AZ (0113) 204 8888 hours Mon–Wed 10–6, Thur 10–8, Fri–Sat 10–7, Sun 11–5
• 21 New Cathedral Street, Manchester M1 1AD (0161) 828 8888 hours Mon–Fri 10–8, Sat 9–7, Sun 11–5
• 27 Philadelphia Street, Quakers Friars, Cabot Circus, Bristol BS1 3BZ (0117) 916 8880 hours Mon–Wed 10–6, Thur
10–8, Fri–Sat 10–7, Sun 11–5

• Dundrum Town Centre, Sandyford Road, Dublin 16, +353 (0) 1291 0420 hours Mon–Tues 10–7, Wed–Fri 10–9, Sat 10–7, Sun 11–7

website www.harveynichols.com cards AmEx, Maestro, MasterCard, Visa. M T

✪ *Sought-after producers and cult fine wines, especially from France, Italy and California.*

Haynes Hanson & Clark

Sheep Street, Stow-on-the-Wold, Gloucestershire GL54 1AA (01451) 870808 fax (01451) 870508
hours Mon–Fri 9–6, Sat 9–5.30

• 7 Elystan Street, London SW3 3NT (020) 7584 7927 fax (020) 7584 7967 hours Mon–Fri 9–7, Sat 9–4.30
email stow@hhandc.co.uk or london@hhandc.co.uk website www.hhandc.co.uk cards Maestro, MasterCard, Switch, Visa discounts 10% unsplit case delivery Free for 1 case or more in central London and areas covered by Stow-on-the-Wold van; elsewhere 1 case £15.60, 2–3 cases £9.75 per case, 4 or more cases £8.10 per case, free on orders over £650 en primeur Bordeaux, Burgundy. M T

✪ *Known for its subtle, elegant wines: top-notch Burgundy is the main focus of the list, but other French regions are well represented, and there's interesting stuff from Spain, Italy, Australia and New Zealand.*

Hedley Wright

• The Hitchin (Wyevale) Centre, Cambridge Road, Hitchin, Hertfordshire SG4 0JT (01462) 431110 fax (01462) 422983
hours Tues–Fri 11–7, Sat 10–7, Sun 11–5
email sales@hedleywright.co.uk website www.hedleywright.co.uk cards AmEx, Maestro, MasterCard, Visa
delivery £5 per delivery, free for orders over £100 minimum order 1 bottle

✪ *A good all-round list, especially strong in Australia, France, Italy, Spain and South Africa.*

Hicks & Don

17 Kingsmead Business Park, Shaftesbury Road, Gillingham, Dorset SP8 5FB (01747) 824292 fax (01747) 826963
email mailbox@hicksanddon.co.uk website www.hicksanddon.co.uk hours Mon–Fri 9–6
cards Maestro, MasterCard, Visa discounts Negotiable delivery Free over £100, otherwise £7.50 per case in UK mainland minimum order 1 case en primeur Bordeaux, Burgundy, Chablis, Chile, Italy, Port, Rhône. C G M T

✪ *Subtle, well-made wines that go with food, particularly French wines. Still plenty of choice under £10.*

The following services are available where indicated: C = cellarage **G** = glass hire/loan **M** = mail/online order **T** = tastings and talks

Jeroboams (incorporating Laytons)

head office 7–9 Elliot's Place, London N1 8HX (020) 7288 8888 fax (020) 7359 2616 hours Mon–Fri 9–5.30
shops 50–52 Elizabeth Street, London SW1W 9PB (020) 7730 8108
● 20 Davies Street, London W1K 3DT (020) 7499 1015 ● 13 Elgin Crescent, London W11 2JA (020) 7229 0527
● 29 Heath Street, London NW3 6TR (020) 7435 6845 ● 96 Holland Park Avenue, London W11 3RB (020) 7727 9359
● 6 Pont Street, London SW1X 9EL (020) 7235 1612 ● 1 St John's Wood High Street, London NW8 7NG (020) 7722 4020
● 56 Walton Street, London SW3 1RB (020) 7589 2020
● Mr Christian's Delicatessen, 11 Elgin Crescent, London W11 2JA (020) 7229 0501
● Milroy's of Soho, 3 Greek Street, London W1D 4NX (020) 7437 2385 (whisky and wine)
email sales@jeroboams.co.uk website www.jeroboams.co.uk hours shops Mon–Sat 9.30/10–7 (may vary)
cards AmEx, Maestro, MasterCard, Visa delivery Free for orders over £285, otherwise £17.25 en primeur Bordeaux,
Burgundy, Rhône. C G M T
✪ Wide-ranging list of affordable and enjoyable wines, especially good in France, Italy, Australia and New Zealand.
Fine foods, especially cheeses and olive oils, are available in the Holland Park and Mr Christian's Delicatessen shops.

S H Jones

27 High Street, Banbury, Oxfordshire OX16 5EW (01295) 251179 fax (01295) 272352 email banbury@shjones.com
● 9 Market Square, Bicester, Oxfordshire OX26 6AA (01869) 322448 email bicester@shjones.com
● The Cellar Shop, 2 Riverside, Tramway Road, Banbury, Oxfordshire OX16 5TU (01295) 672296 fax (01295) 259560
email retail@shjones.com ● 121 Regent Street, Leamington Spa, Warwickshire CV32 4NU (01926) 315609
email leamington@shjones.com website www.shjones.com hours Mon-Sat 9.30-5.30 cards Maestro, MasterCard, Visa
delivery Free for 12 bottles of wine/spirits or total value over £100 within 30-mile radius of shops, otherwise £9.75 per
case en primeur Burgundy, Port, New Zealand, South Africa, Australia, Italy, Spain. G M T
✪ Wide-ranging list with good stuff from France, Italy and Spain, exciting New World selection, and plenty of tasty wine for
less than £10.

Justerini & Brooks

mail order 61 St James's Street, London SW1A 1LZ (020) 7484 6400 fax (020) 7484 6499
email justorders@justerinis.com website www.justerinis.com hours Mon–Fri 9–5.30 cards Maestro, MasterCard, Visa
delivery Free for unmixed cases over £250, otherwise £15 + VAT in UK mainland minimum order 1 case
en primeur Alsace, Bordeaux, Burgundy, Italy, Spain, Loire, Rhône, Germany. C M T
✪ Superb list of top-quality wines from Europe's classic regions, as well as some excellent New World choices.

Laithwaites Wine

mail order New Aquitaine House, Exeter Way, Theale, Reading, Berkshire RG7 4PL **order line** 0845 194 7700
fax 0845 194 7766 **email** orders@laithwaites.co.uk **website** www.laithwaites.co.uk **hours** Mon–Fri 8.30–9, Sat 9–8,
Sun 9–6 **cards** AmEx, Diners, Maestro, MasterCard, Visa **discounts** On unmixed cases of 6 or 12
delivery £7.99 per delivery address **minimum order** no minimum order but most offers available in 6 or 12 bottle cases
(mixed and unmixed)
en primeur Australia, Bordeaux, Burgundy, Rhône, Rioja. **C M T**
• Flagship store: The Arch, 219–221 Stoney Street, London SE1 9AA (020) 7407 6378 **fax** (020) 7407 5411
email thearch@laithwaiteswine.com **hours** Mon–Thur 10–7, Fri 10–10, Sat 10–8, Sun 12–6
✪ *Mail order specialist with new flagship store just off Borough Market and 10 other shops in the South-East and the
Midlands. Extensive selection of wines from France, Australia, Spain, Italy and elsewhere.*

Lay & Wheeler

mail order Holton Park, Holton St Mary, Suffolk CO7 6NN (01473) 313300 **fax** (01473) 313264
email sales@laywheeler.com **website** www.laywheeler.com **hours** (Order office) Mon–Fri 8.30–5.30
cards AmEx, Maestro, MasterCard, Visa **delivery** £9.95; free for orders over £200
en primeur Bordeaux, Burgundy, Port (some vintages), Rhône, Spain, Portugal, Germany, Austria, Champagne. **C M T**
✪ *A must-have list with first-class Bordeaux and Burgundy to satisfy the most demanding drinker, and plenty more besides.
En primeur and fine wines are two core strengths here.*

Lea & Sandeman

170 Fulham Road, London SW10 9PR (020) 7244 0522 **fax** (020) 7244 0533
• 51 High Street, Barnes, London SW13 9LN (020) 8878 8643 • 211 Kensington Church Street, London W8 7LX
(020) 7221 1982 • 167 Chiswick High Road, London W4 2DR (020) 8995 7355 **email** info@leaandsandeman.co.uk
website www.leaandsandeman.co.uk **hours** Mon–Sat 10–8 **cards** AmEx, Maestro, MasterCard, Visa
discounts 5–15% by case, other discounts on 10 cases or more **delivery** London £10 for less than £100, otherwise
free, and free to UK mainland south of Perth on orders over £250, otherwise £15
en primeur Bordeaux, Burgundy, Italy. **C G M T**
✪ *Burgundy and Italy take precedence here, and there's a succession of excellent names, chosen with great care by
Charles Lea and Patrick Sandeman. Bordeaux has wines at all price levels, and there are short but fascinating ranges from
the USA, Spain, Australia and New Zealand.*

Liberty Wines

mail order Unit D18, The Food Market, New Covent Garden, London SW8 5LL (020) 7720 5350 fax (020) 7720 6158
email order@libertywines.co.uk website www.libertywines.co.uk hours Mon–Fri 9–5.30 cards Maestro, MasterCard,
Visa delivery Free to mainland UK minimum order 12 x 75cl bottles. M

✪ *Italy rules, with superb wines from pretty well all the best producers. Liberty are the UK agents for most of their producers, so if you're interested in Italian wines this should be your first port of call. Also top names from Australia and elsewhere.*

Linlithgow Wines

Crossford, Station Road, Linlithgow, West Lothian EH49 6BW (01506) 848821 email jrobmcd@aol.com
website www.linlithgowwines.co.uk hours flexible (please phone first) cards None: cash, cheque or bank transfer only
delivery £5 locally; elsewhere in UK £9 for 1 case, £15 for 2 cases and £5 per case thereafter. G M T

✪ *Terrific list of French wines, many imported direct from family-run vineyards in southern France.*

O W Loeb & Co

mail order 3 Archie Street, off Tanner Street, London SE1 3JT (020) 7234 0385 fax (020) 7357 0440
email finewine@owloeb.com website www.owloeb.com hours Mon–Fri 8.30–5.30 cards Maestro, MasterCard, Visa
discounts 24 bottles and above delivery Free for 24 bottles and above except north of Glasgow and Edinburgh
minimum order 12 bottles en primeur Burgundy, Bordeaux, Rhône, Germany (Mosel). C M T

✪ *Burgundy, the Rhône, Loire and Germany stand out, with top producers galore. Then there are Loeb's new discoveries from Spain and the New World, especially New Zealand and South Africa.*

Maison du Vin

Moor Hill, Hawkhurst, Kent TN18 4PF (01580) 753487 fax (01580) 755627 email kvgriffin@aol.com
website www.maison-du-vin.co.uk hours Mon 10–4, Tue–Fri 10–5, Sat 10–6 cards Access, AmEx, Maestro,
MasterCard, Visa delivery Free locally; UK mainland at cost en primeur Bordeaux. C G M T

✪ *As the name suggests, the focus is on French wines, and interesting wines, not brands. There is some good stuff from Australia and Chile – at prices from about £6 upwards. There's a monthly themed 'wine school' or you can book personal tutored tastings.*

Majestic (see also Wine and Beer World)

head office Majestic House, Otterspool Way, Watford, Herts WD25 8WW (01923) 298200

fax (01923) 819105; 165 stores nationwide email info@majestic.co.uk website www.majestic.co.uk
hours Mon–Fri 10–8, Sat 9–7, Sun 10–5 (may vary) cards AmEx, Diners, Maestro, MasterCard, Visa
delivery Free UK mainland if you buy 12 or more bottles minimum order (in-store) 1 mixed case (6 bottles)
en primeur Bordeaux, Port, Burgundy. G M T
✪ *One of the best places to buy Champagne, with a good range and good discounts for buying in quantity.
Loads of interesting and reasonably priced stuff, especially from France, Germany and the New World.*

Marks & Spencer
head office Waterside House, 35 North Wharf Road, London W2 1NW (020) 7935 4422 fax (020) 7487 2679;
600 licensed stores website www.marksandspencer.com hours Variable
discounts Variable, a selection of 10 different Wines of the Month, buy any 6 and save 10% in selected stores. M T
✪ *M&S works with top producers around the world to create its impressive list of own-label wines. All the wines are
exclusive and unique to M&S, selected by their in-house winemaking team.*

Martinez Wines
35 The Grove, Ilkley, Leeds, West Yorkshire LS29 9NJ (01943) 600000 fax 0870 922 3940
email shop@martinez.co.uk website www.martinez.co.uk hours Sun 12–6, Mon–Wed 10–8, Thur–Fri 10–9, Sat
9.30–6 cards AmEx, Maestro, MasterCard, Visa discounts 5% on 6 bottles or more, 10% on orders over £150
delivery Free local delivery, otherwise £15.50 per case mainland UK en primeur Bordeaux, Burgundy. C G M T
✪ *From a wide-ranging list, I'd single out the selections from France, Italy, Spain, Australia, Argentina and South Africa.*

Millésima
mail order 87 Quai de Paludate, CS 11691, 33050 Bordeaux Cedex, France (00 33) 5 57 80 88 08
fax (00 33) 5 57 80 88 19 Freephone 0800 917 0352 website www.millesima.com hours Mon–Fri 8–5.30
cards AmEx, Diners, Maestro, MasterCard, Visa delivery For bottled wines, free to single UK addresses for orders
exceeding £500. Otherwise, a charge of £20 will be applied. For en primeur wines, free to single UK addresses.
en primeur Bordeaux, Burgundy, Rhône. M T
✪ *Wine comes direct from the châteaux to Millésima's 200-year-old cellars, where 2.5 million bottles are stored. Bordeaux
and Burgundy are the core strengths, with vintages going back to the 1980s and including a large selection of magnums,
double magnums, jeroboams (5 litres) and imperiales (6 litres). Plus a sprinkling of established names from Burgundy,
Alsace, the Rhône and Champagne.*

Montrachet

mail order 11 Catherine Place, London SW1E 6DX (020) 7821 1337 email charles@montrachetwine.com
website www.montrachetwine.com hours Mon–Fri 8.30–5.30 cards AmEx, Maestro, MasterCard, Visa
delivery England and Wales £15, free for 3 or more cases; for Scotland ring for details
minimum order 1 unmixed case en primeur Bordeaux, Burgundy. C M T
✪ *Impressive Burgundies are the main attraction here, but there are also some very good Rhônes, and Bordeaux is excellent at all price levels.*

Moreno Wines

11 Marylands Road, London W9 2DU (020) 7286 0678 fax (020) 7286 0513 email merchant@moreno-wines.co.uk
website www.morenowinedirect.com hours Mon–Fri 4–8, Sat 12–8 cards AmEx, Maestro, MasterCard, Visa
discounts 10% on 1 or more cases delivery Up to 1 case £8, up to 2 cases £10, free thereafter. M T
✪ *Specialist in Spanish wines, from everyday drinking to fine and rare wines from older vintages, with a few well-chosen additions from Australia, Italy and elsewhere.*

Wm Morrisons Supermarkets

head office Hilmore House, Gain Lane, Bradford, West Yorkshire BD3 7DL 0845 611 5000 fax 0845 611 6801
456 licensed branches customer service 0845 611 6111; Mon–Fri 8–6.30, Sat 9–5 website www.morrisons.co.uk
hours Variable, generally Mon–Sat 7–9, Sun 10–4 cards AmEx, Delta, Maestro, MasterCard, Style, Visa Electron. G T
✪ *Inexpensive, often tasty wines, and if you're prepared to trade up a little there's some really good stuff here.*

New Zealand House of Wine

mail order/online based near Petworth, Surrey email info@nzhouseofwine.com website www.nzhouseofwine.co.uk
order freephone 0800 085 6273 enquiries (01428) 70 77 33 fax (01428) 70 77 66
hours Mon–Fri, UK office hours cards AmEx, Delta, Maestro, MasterCard, Visa, Visa Debit
discounts often available on high-volume orders (60+ bottles) for parties, weddings and other events
delivery UK mainland only: free delivery for orders above £200, £5.99 for orders above £100, £9.59 for orders less than £100. M
✪ *Impressive list of over 300 New Zealand wines, with plenty under £10 and some really fine stuff around £20 and over.*

The following services are available where indicated: **C** = cellarage **G** = glass hire/loan **M** = mail/online order **T** = tastings and talks

James Nicholson

7/9 Killyleagh Street, Crossgar, Co. Down, Northern Ireland BT30 9DQ (028) 4483 0091 fax (028) 4483 0028
email shop@jnwine.com website www.jnwine.com hours Mon–Sat 10–7 cards Maestro, MasterCard, Visa
discounts 10% mixed case delivery Free (1 case or more) in Eire and Northern Ireland; UK mainland £10.95,
2 cases £15.95 en primeur Bordeaux, Burgundy, California, Rioja, Rhône. C G M T
❂ *Well-chosen list mainly from small, committed growers around the world. Bordeaux, Rhône and southern France are
slightly ahead of the field, there's a good selection of Burgundy and some excellent drinking from Germany and Spain.*

Nickolls & Perks

37 Lower High Street, Stourbridge, West Midlands DY8 1TA (01384) 394518 fax (01384) 440786
email sales@nickollsandperks.co.uk website www.nickollsandperks.co.uk hours Tues–Fri 10.30–5.30, Sat 10.30–5
cards Maestro, MasterCard, Visa discounts negotiable per case delivery £10 per consignment; free over £150
en primeur Bordeaux, Champagne, Port. C G M T
❂ *Established in 1797, Nickolls & Perks have a wide-ranging list – and a terrific website – covering most areas.
Their strength is France. Advice is available to clients wishing to develop their cellars or invest in wine.*

Nidderdale Fine Wines

2a High Street, Pateley Bridge, North Yorkshire HG3 5AW (01423) 711703 email mike@southaustralianwines.com
website www.southaustralianwines.com hours Tues–Sat 10–6 cards Maestro, MasterCard, Visa
discounts 5% case discount on shop purchases for 12+ bottles delivery £5 per 12-bottle case in England, Wales
and southern Scotland. Single bottle delivery available. G M T
❂ *Specialist in South Australia, with around 300 wines broken down into regions. Also 350 or so wines from the rest of the
world. Look out for online offers and winemaker dinners.*

Noble Rot Wine Warehouses

Willowbrook Garden Centre, 222 Stourbridge Road, Catfield, Bromsgrove, Worcestershire B61 0BW
email info@noble-rot.co.uk website www.noble-rot.co.uk hours Mon–Sat 9.30–5.30
cards Maestro, MasterCard, Visa discounts Various delivery Free within 10-mile radius. G T
❂ *Australia, Italy, France and Spain feature strongly in a frequently changing array of more than 400 wines, mostly at
£10–15. Also a selection of fine wines and Champagnes.*

O'Briens

head office 33 Spruce Avenue, Stillorgan Industrial Park, Co. Dublin, Ireland (01) 269 3139
fax 01 269 7480; 30 stores **email** sales@obrienswines.ie; info@obrienswines.ie **website** www.wine.ie
hours Mon–Sat 10.30am–10pm, Sun 12.30–10pm **cards** AmEx, MasterCard, Visa **delivery** €10 per case anywhere in
Ireland (minimum order 6 bottles); free for orders over €200 **en primeur** Bordeaux. **G M T**
✪ *Family-owned drinks retailer, which could well claim to be the best of the chains in Ireland. Imports directly from over 75 wineries worldwide.*

Old Chapel Cellars

The Old Chapel, Millpool, Truro, Cornwall TR1 1EX (01872) 270545 **email** jamie@oldchapelcellars.co.uk
website www.oldchapelcellars.co.uk **hours** Mon–Sat 10–6 **cards** Maestro, MasterCard, Visa
delivery £7.99 per case UK mainland; free for orders over £95. **G M T**
✪ *Excellent, knowledgeable list that specializes in Spain and Portugal, plus wines from all over the world.*

The Oxford Wine Company

The Wine Warehouse, Witney Road, Standlake, Oxfordshire OX29 7PR (01865) 301144 **fax** (01865) 301155
email orders@oxfordwine.co.uk **website** www.oxfordwine.co.uk **hours** Mon–Sat 9–7, Sun 11–4
• 165 Botley Road, Oxford OX2 0PB (01865) 249500 **hours** Mon–Sat 10–8, Sun 11–6
• Units 1 & 2, Baytree Court, The Chippings, Tetbury, Gloucestershire GL8 8ET (01666) 500429
hours Mon–Sat 9.30–6.30 **cards** AmEx, Diners, Maestro, MasterCard, Visa **discounts** 5% discount on a case of 12
delivery Free locally; national delivery £9.99 for any amount **en primeur** Bordeaux. **G M T**
✪ *A good selection from the classic regions and the New World, from bargain basement prices to expensive fine wines.*

OZ WINES

mail order Oz Wines, Freepost RSHB-HHTE-CZGH, Berkshire SL6 5AQ (0845) 4501261 **email** sales@ozwines.co.uk
website www.ozwines.co.uk **hours** Mon–Fri 9.30–7 **cards** Almost all major credit cards **delivery** Free
minimum order 1 mixed case. **M T**
✪ *Australian wines made by small wineries and real people – with the thrilling flavours that Australians do better than anyone.*

Penistone Court Wine Cellars

The Railway Station, Penistone, Sheffield, South Yorkshire S36 6HP (01226) 766037
email orders@pcwine.plus.com **website** www.penistonewines.co.uk **hours** Tues–Fri 10–6, Sat 10–3 **cards** Maestro,

MasterCard, Visa **delivery** Free locally, rest of UK mainland charged at cost **minimum order** no minimum order **G M**
✪ *A well-balanced list, with something from just about everywhere, mostly from familiar names.*

Philglas & Swiggot

21 Northcote Road, Battersea, London SW11 1NG (020) 7924 4494

• 64 Hill Rise, Richmond, London TW10 6UB (020) 8332 6031

• 22 New Quebec Street, Marylebone, London W1H 7SB (020) 7402 0002

email info@philglas-swiggot.co.uk **website** www.philglas-swiggot.com **hours** Mon–Sat 11–7, Sun 12–5
cards AmEx, Maestro, MasterCard, Visa **discounts** 5% per case **delivery** Free 1 case locally, or £5 elsewhere. **G M**
✪ *Excellent selections from Australia, Italy, France and Austria – interesting, characterful wines rather than blockbuster brands. Subscriber's club with estate wines, bin ends and limited allocation wines.*

Christopher Piper Wines

1 Silver Street, Ottery St Mary, Devon EX11 1DB (01404) 814139 **fax** (01404) 812100
email sales@christopherpiperwines.co.uk **website** www.christopherpiperwines.co.uk
hours Mon–Fri 8.30–5.30, Sat 9–4.30 **cards** Maestro, MasterCard, Visa **discounts** 5% mixed case, 10% 3 or more
cases **delivery** £9.20 for 1 case then £4.90 for each case, free delivery within van areas and for orders over £220 inc
VAT **en primeur** Bordeaux, Burgundy, Rhône. **C G M T**
✪ *Huge range of well-chosen wines that reflect a sense of place and personality, with lots of information to help you make up your mind.*

Terry Platt Wine Merchants

Council Street West, Llandudno LL30 1ED (01492) 874099 **fax** (01492) 874788 **email** sales@terryplattwines.co.uk
website www.terryplattwines.co.uk **hours** Mon–Fri 8.30–5.30 **cards** Access, Maestro, MasterCard, Visa
delivery Free locally and UK mainland 5 cases or more **minimum order** 1 mixed case. **G M T**
✪ *A wide-ranging list with a sprinkling of good growers from most regions.*

Portland Wine Company

152a Ashley Road, Hale, Altrincham, Cheshire WA15 9SA (0161) 928 0357 **fax** (0161) 905 1291

• 54 London Road, Alderley Edge, Cheshire SK5 7DX (01625) 590919

• 82 Chester Road, Macclesfield, Cheshire SK11 8DA (01625) 616147

• 45–47 Compstall Road, Marple Bridge, Cheshire SK6 5HG (0161) 4260155

• 44 High Street, Tarporley, Cheshire CW6 0DX (01829) 730762

email info@portlandwine.co.uk **website** www.portlandwine.co.uk **hours** Mon–Fri 10–9, Sat 9–9
cards Maestro, MasterCard, Visa **discounts** 5% on 2 cases or more, 10% on 5 cases or more **delivery** Free for orders over £100 per consignment nationwide, smaller orders at a cost. **en primeur** Bordeaux. **C T**

✪ *Spain, Portugal and Burgundy are specialities and there's a promising-looking list of clarets. Consumer-friendly list with something at every price level from around the world.*

Private Cellar

mail order 51 High Street, Wicken, Cambridgeshire CB7 5XR (01353) 721999 **fax** (01353) 724074
email orders@privatecellar.co.uk **website** www.privatecellar.co.uk **hours** Mon–Fri 8–6 **cards** Delta, Maestro, MasterCard, Visa **delivery** £14.50, or free for orders of 24+ bottles in mainland England and Wales. For Scotland, islands, Northern Ireland and worldwide, phone for quote **en primeur** Bordeaux, Burgundy, Rhône, Germany, Port, California. **C M T**

✪ *Friendly, personal wine advice is part of the service; wines are predominantly French, with lots of 'everyday claret' at £10–15.*

Quaff Fine Wine Merchant

139–141 Portland Road, Hove BN3 5QJ (01273) 820320 **fax** (01273) 820326 **email** sales@quaffit.com
website www.quaffit.com **hours** Mon–Sat 9–9, Sun 10–9 **cards** Access, Maestro, MasterCard, Visa
discounts 10% mixed case **delivery** Next working day nationwide, charge depends on order value. **C G M T**

✪ *Extensive and keenly priced list organized by grape variety rather than by country.*

Raeburn Fine Wines

21–23 Comely Bank Road, Edinburgh EH4 1DS (0131) 343 1159 **fax** (0131) 332 5166
email sales@raeburnfinewines.com **website** www.raeburnfinewines.com **hours** Mon–Sat 10–6
cards AmEx, Maestro, MasterCard, Visa **discounts** 5% unsplit case, 2.5% mixed case **delivery** Free local area 1 or more cases (usually); elsewhere at cost **en primeur** Australia, Bordeaux, Burgundy, California, Germany, Italy, Languedoc-Roussillon, Loire, New Zealand, Rhône. **G M T**

✪ *Carefully chosen list, mainly from small growers. Italy and France – especially Burgundy – are specialities, with Germany, Austria and northern Spain close behind, as well as selected Port and sought-after California wines such as Shafer Vineyards and Turley Cellars.*

> **The following services are available where indicated: C** = cellarage **G** = glass hire/loan **M** = mail/online order **T** = tastings and talks

The Real Wine Company

mail order c/o Pinewood Nurseries, Wexham Street, Stoke Poges, Buckinghamshire SL3 6NB (01753) 664190
email mark@therealwineco.co.uk website www.therealwineco.co.uk cards Delta, Maestro, MasterCard, Visa, AmEx
delivery £6.99 per order, orders over £250 free minimum order 1 mixed case.
✪ *Owner Mark Hughes has based his list entirely on his personal taste – check it out and see if you agree with his lively tasting notes. Plenty of good-value wines. There are also wine and food matches, with recipe suggestions.*

Reid Wines

The Mill, Marsh Lane, Hallatrow, Nr Bristol BS39 6EB (01761) 452645 fax (01761) 453642 email reidwines@aol.com
hours Mon–Fri 9–5.30 cards Access, Maestro, MasterCard, Visa (3% charge)
delivery Free within 25 miles of Hallatrow (Bristol), and in central London for orders over 2 cases
en primeur Claret. C G M T
✪ *A mix of great old wines, some old duds and splendid current stuff. Italy, USA, Australia, port and Madeira look tremendous.*

Reserve Wines

176 Burton Road, West Didsbury, Manchester M20 1LH (0161) 438 0101 email sales@reservewines.co.uk
website www.reservewines.co.uk hours Mon–Fri 12–9, Sat 11–9, Sun 12–7 cards Delta, Maestro, MasterCard, Solo, Switch, Visa delivery Starts from £8.50. G M T
✪ *Award-winning wine specialist established in 2003 and focusing on making the world of wine accessible and fun.*

Howard Ripley

mail order 18 Madrid Road, London SW13 9PD (020) 8877 3065 fax (020) 8877 0029
email info@howardripley.com website www.howardripley.com hours Mon–Fri 9–6
cards Maestro, MasterCard, Visa delivery Minimum charge £11.50 + VAT, free UK mainland on orders over £600 ex-VAT
en primeur Burgundy, Germany, Oregon, New Zealand, Switzerland. C M T
✪ *A must-have list for serious Burgundy lovers; expensive but not excessive, and including a great backlist of older vintages. The German range is also excellent.*

Roberson

348 Kensington High Street, London W14 8NS (020) 7371 2121 fax (020) 7371 4010
email enquiries@roberson.co.uk website www.robersonwinemerchant.co.uk; www.roberson.co.uk

hours Mon–Sat 10–8, Sun 12–6 cards Access, AmEx, Maestro, MasterCard, Visa discounts up to a third off unsplit cases, 10% mixed cases delivery Free delivery in the UK on orders over £200, otherwise charges apply en primeur Bordeaux, Port. C G M T

✪ *Fine and rare wines, sold by the bottle. All of France is excellent; so is Italy and port. With friendly, knowledgeable staff, the shop is well worth a visit.*

The RSJ Wine Company

33 Coin Street, London SE1 9NR (020) 7928 4554 fax (020) 7928 9768 email tom.king@rsj.uk.com website www.rsj.uk.com hours Mon–Fri 9–6, answering machine at other times cards AmEx, Maestro, MasterCard, Visa delivery Free central London, minimum 1 case; England and Wales (per case), £14.10 1 case, £10.25 2 cases or more. G M T

✪ *A roll-call of great Loire names.*

SA Wines Online

head office/warehouse 15 Windsor Park, 50 Windsor Avenue, Merton, London SW19 2TJ 0845 456 2365 fax 0845 456 2366 email customers@sawinesonline.co.uk website www.sawinesonline.co.uk hours Mon–Fri 9–5.30 cards AmEx, Maestro, MasterCard, Visa delivery £6.99 per delivery address in UK mainland; check website for charges to Isle of Wight, Scottish highlands and islands, Northern Ireland minimum order 1 mixed case discounts £10 off first order (over £60); loyalty scheme. M T

✪ *Your first stop for South African wines in the UK – and if they don't list the wine you want they may still be able to help you get it. The website is full of information on South Africa's wine regions and producers, plus food and wine matching. Occasional warehouse tastings and events.*

Sainsbury's

head office 33 Holborn, London EC1N 2HT (020) 7695 6000 customer service 0800 636262; 876 stores website www.sainsburys.co.uk online groceries helpline 0800 328 1700 hours Variable, some 24 hrs, locals Mon–Sat 7–11, Sun 10 or 11–4 cards AmEx, Maestro, MasterCard, Visa discounts 5% for 6 bottles or more. G M T

✪ *A collection to cater for bargain hunters as well as lovers of good-value wine higher up the scale. They've expanded their Taste the Difference range and got some top producers on board.*

The following services are available where indicated: C = cellarage **G** = glass hire/loan **M** = mail/online order **T** = tastings and talks

The Sampler

266 Upper Street, London N1 2UQ (020) 7226 9500 fax (020) 7226 6555 email jamie@thesampler.co.uk
website www.thesampler.co.uk hours Mon–Sat 11.30–9
• 35 Thurloe Place, London SW7 2HP hours Mon–Sat 11.30–9, Sun 11.30–7
cards Maestro, MasterCard, Visa delivery Free locally for minimum 1 case; £10 elsewhere on UK mainland. Next day and
Sat deliveries at extra cost discounts 10% for 6 bottles or more, or to online orders over £75. G M T
✪ *The future of wine retailing? 1200 wines in the range (strengths include older vintages of Bordeaux and Rioja, sherry and grower Champagnes), long opening hours, email newsletters and Enomatic sampling machines allowing you to taste up to 80 wines before buying. Regular tastings and courses.*

Savage Selection

The Ox House, Market Place, Northleach, Cheltenham, Glos GL54 3EG (01451) 860896 fax (01451) 860996
• The Ox House Shop and Wine Bar at same address (01451) 860680 email wine@savageselection.co.uk
website www.savageselection.co.uk hours Office Mon–Fri 9–6; shop and wine bar Tue–Sat 10–10 cards Maestro,
MasterCard, Visa delivery Free locally for orders over £100; elsewhere on UK mainland free for orders over £250;
smaller orders £10 + VAT for 1 case and £5 + VAT for each additional case en primeur Bordeaux. C G M T
✪ *Owner Mark Savage MW seeks out wines of genuine originality and personality from small family estates. France is the mainstay, alongside wines from Slovenia, Austria, Oregon and elsewhere.*

Seckford Wines

Dock Lane, Melton, Suffolk IP12 1PE (01394) 446622 fax (01394) 446633 email sales@seckfordwines.co.uk
website www.seckfordwines.co.uk cards Maestro, MasterCard, Visa delivery £14.40 per consignment in UK mainland;
elsewhere at cost minimum order 1 mixed case en primeur Bordeaux, Burgundy. C M
✪ *Bordeaux, Burgundy, Champagne and the Rhône are the stars of this list, with some excellent older vintages. Serious stuff from Italy and Spain, too.*

Selfridges

400 Oxford Street, London W1A 1AB 0800 123 400 (for all stores) hours London Mon–Sat 9.30–8.30, Sun 12–6
• Upper Mall East, Bullring, Birmingham B5 4BP Mon–Fri 10–8 (Thur 10–9), Sat 9–8, Sun 11–5
• 1 Exchange Square, Manchester M3 1BD • The Trafford Centre, Manchester M17 8DA hours both Manchester
branches Mon–Fri 10–8 (Thur 10–9), Sat 9–8, Sun 11–5
email wineshop@selfridges.co.uk website www.selfridges.co.uk cards AmEx, Maestro, MasterCard, Visa

discounts 10% case discount delivery £10 within 3 working days, UK mainland. T

❂ *Strong fine wine list with a wide range of classic wines, from Bordeaux through to Tokaji from Hungary. Great selection for gifts – as well as less expensive bottles, there are plenty of highly sought-after wines at £500-plus and you can even buy a bottle of Screaming Eagle, one of Napa's hottest properties, for £2400. Regular tastings.*

Somerfield See Co-operative.

Sommelier Wine Co
23 St George's Esplanade, St Peter Port, Guernsey, Channel Islands GY1 2BG (01481) 721677 fax (01481) 716818
hours Mon–Sat 9.15–5.30, except Fri 9.15–6 cards Maestro, MasterCard, Visa discounts 5% 1 case or more
delivery Free locally (minimum 1 mixed case); being outside the European Community and with Customs restrictions means that the shipping of wine to the UK mainland is not possible. G T

❂ *An excellent list, with interesting, unusual wines.*

Stainton Wines
1 Station Yard, Station Road, Kendal, Cumbria LA9 6BT (01539) 731886 fax (01539) 730396
email admin@stainton-wines.co.uk website www.stainton-wines.co.uk hours Mon–Fri 9–5.30, Sat 9–4.30
cards Maestro, MasterCard, Visa discounts 5% mixed case delivery Free Cumbria and North Lancashire;
elsewhere (per case) £13 1 case, more than 1 case variable. G M T

❂ *The list includes some great Bordeaux, interesting Burgundy, and leading names from Italy and Chile.*

Stevens Garnier
47 West Way, Botley, Oxford OX2 OJF (01865) 263303 fax (01865) 791594 email shop@stevensgarnier.co.uk
website www.stevensgarnier.co.uk hours Mon–Thur 10–6, Fri 10–7, Sat 10–5 cards AmEx, MasterCard, Visa
discounts 10% on 12 bottles delivery Free locally. G M T

❂ *Regional France is a strength: this is one of the few places in the UK you can buy wine from Savoie. Likewise, there are interesting choices from Portugal, Australia, Chile and Canada.*

Stone, Vine & Sun
mail order No. 13 Humphrey Farms, Hazeley Road, Twyford, Winchester, Hampshire SO21 1QA (01962) 712351
fax (01962) 717545 email sales@stonevine.co.uk website www.stonevine.co.uk hours Mon–Fri 9–6, Sat 9.30–4
cards Access, Maestro, MasterCard, Visa discounts 5% on an unmixed case delivery £5.50 for 1st case, £8.50 for

2 cases, free for orders over £250. Prices vary for Scottish Highlands, islands and Northern Ireland. **G M T**

✪ *Lovely list marked by enthusiasm and passion for the subject. Lots of interesting stuff from France, especially the Rhône, Burgundy, Languedoc-Roussillon and the Loire. South Africa and South America are other strong areas, plus there are wines from Germany, New Zealand, the USA and elsewhere.*

Sunday Times Wine Club

mail order New Aquitaine House, Exeter Way, Theale, Reading, Berkshire RG7 4PL **order line** 0845 217 9122 **fax** 0845 217 9144 **email** orders@sundaytimeswineclub.co.uk **website** www.sundaytimeswineclub.co.uk **hours** Mon–Fri 8.30–9, Sat–Sun 9–6 **cards** AmEx, Diners, Maestro, MasterCard, Visa **delivery** £5.99 per order **en primeur** Australia, Bordeaux, Burgundy, Rhône. **C M T**

✪ *Essentially the same as Laithwaites (see page 171). The Club runs tours and tasting events for its members.*

Swig

mail order/online 188 Sutton Court Road, London W4 3HR (020) 8995 7060 or freephone 08000 272 272 **fax** (020) 8995 6195 **email** wine@swig.co.uk **website** www.swig.co.uk **cards** Amex, MasterCard, Switch, Visa **delivery** Free for orders over £90 **en primeur** Bordeaux, Burgundy, South Africa. **C G M T**

✪ *Seriously good wines sold in an unserious way. For instant recommendations there's a list of 'current favourites' organized in price bands; there's lots between £8 and £20 and the list covers pretty much everything you might want.*

T & W Wines

5 Station Way, Brandon, Suffolk IP27 0BH (01842) 814414 **fax** (01842) 819967 **email** contact@tw-wines.com **website** www.tw-wines.com **hours** Mon–Fri 9–5.30, occasional Sat 9.30–1 **cards** AmEx, MasterCard, Visa **delivery** (Most areas) 7–23 bottles £18.95 + VAT, 2 or more cases free **en primeur** Burgundy. **C G M T**

✪ *A good list, particularly if you're looking for interesting wines from Burgundy, Rhône, Alsace or the Loire, but prices are not especially low.*

Tanners

26 Wyle Cop, Shrewsbury, Shropshire SY1 1XD (01743) 234500 **fax** (01743) 234501 **hours** Mon–Sat 9–6
• 36 High Street, Bridgnorth WV16 4DB (01746) 763148 **fax** (01746) 769798 **hours** Mon–Sat 9–5.30
• 4 St Peter's Square, Hereford HR1 2PG (01432) 272044 **fax** (01432) 263316 **hours** Mon–Sat 9–5.30
• Council Street West, Llandudno LL30 1ED (01492) 874099 **fax** (01492) 874788 **hours** Mon–Fri 9–5.30
• Severn Farm Enterprise Park, Welshpool SY21 7DF (01938) 552542 **fax** (01938) 556565

hours Mon–Fri 9–5.30, Sat 9–1

email sales@tanners-wines.co.uk **website** www.tanners-wines.co.uk **cards** Maestro, MasterCard, Visa

discounts 5% 1 mixed case, 7.5% 3 mixed cases (cash & collection); 5% for 2 mixed cases, 7.5% for 4 (mail order)

delivery Free on orders over £90 to one address, otherwise £7.95

en primeur Bordeaux, Burgundy, Rhône, Germany, Port, occasionally others. **C G M T**

✪ *Outstanding, award-winning merchant: Bordeaux, Burgundy and Germany are terrific – and there's excellent stuff from elsewhere, as well as port, madeira and sherry.*

Terroir Languedoc Wines

mail order/online Treetops, Grassington Road, Skipton, North Yorkshire BD23 1LL (01756) 700512 **fax** (01756) 797856

email enquiries@terroirlanguedoc.co.uk **website** www.terroirlanguedoc.co.uk **hours** Mon–Fri 8–5

cards Maestro, MasterCard, Visa **discount** Mixed case offers available alongside bespoke service. **M T**

✪ *Hand-picked list of wines from interesting growers in one of France's most innovative regions.*

Tesco

head office Tesco House, PO Box 18, Delamare Road, Cheshunt EN8 9SL (01992) 632222 **fax** (01992) 630794

customer service 0800 505555; 1830 licensed branches **email** customer.services@tesco.co.uk

website www.tesco.com **hours** Variable **cards** Maestro, MasterCard, Visa **discounts** 5% on 6 bottles or more. **G M T**

• **online** www.tesco.com/wine **discounts** All cases include a 5% discount to match offers in-store, discounts vary monthly on featured cases **cards** AmEx, Mastercard, Visa, Maestro, Clubcard Plus **minimum order** 1 case (6 bottles), 6 bottles for Champagne **delivery** Choice of next day delivery or convenient 2-hour slots

✪ *A range of 850 wines from everyday drinking to fine wines. Tesco.com/wine has an even greater selection by the case – over 1200 wines and champagnes. New features include a fine wine page and a next day delivery system.*

House of Townend

Wyke Way, Melton West Business Park, Hull, East Yorkshire HU14 3HH (01482) 638888

email sales@houseoftownend.co.uk **website** www.houseoftownend.com **hours** (Cellar door) Mon–Sat 11–7, Sun 12–5

cards AmEx, Maestro, MasterCard, Visa **discounts** 5% per case **delivery** Free 1 case locally, or £5 elsewhere. **C G M T**

✪ *Solid range at all price points, with some very useful mature wines from the classic European areas.*

The following services are available where indicated: C = cellarage **G** = glass hire/loan **M** = mail/online order **T** = tastings and talks

Turville Valley Wines

The Firs, Potter Row, Great Missenden, Bucks HP16 9LT (01494) 868818 **fax** (01494) 868832
email chris@turville-valley-wines.com **website** www.turville-valley-wines.com
hours Mon–Fri 9–5.30 **cards** None **delivery** By arrangement **minimum order** £300 excluding VAT/12 bottles. **C M**
✪ *Top-quality fine and rare wines at trade prices.*

Valvona & Crolla

19 Elm Row, Edinburgh EH7 4AA (0131) 556 6066 **fax** (0131) 556 1668
email wine@valvonacrolla.co.uk **website** www.valvonacrolla.co.uk
hours Shop: Mon–Sat 8.30–6, Sun 10.30–4, Caffe bar: Mon–Sat 8.30–5.30, Sun 10.30–3.30 **cards** AmEx, Maestro,
MasterCard, Visa **discounts** 7% 1–36 bottles, 10% 37+ bottles **delivery** Edinburgh: Free min £30. UK: Free on orders
over £150, otherwise £10; Sat mornings free on orders over £200, otherwise £30. **M T**
✪ *Exciting selection of wines from all over the world, but specializing in Italy. 25 different Italian liqueurs and grappas.*
Branches in Jenners, Edinburgh and Jenners, Loch Lomond.

Villeneuve Wines

1 Venlaw Court, Peebles EH45 8AE (01721) 722500 **fax** (01721) 729922
• 82 High Street, Haddington EH41 3ET (01620) 822224 • 49A Broughton Street, Edinburgh EH1 3RJ (0131) 558 8441
email wines@villeneuvewines.com **website** www.villeneuvewines.com
hours (Peebles) Mon–Sat 10–8, Sun 12–5.30; (Haddington) Mon–Sat 10–7; (Edinburgh) Mon–Wed 12–10, Thur–Sat
10–10, Sun 12–10
cards AmEx, Maestro, MasterCard, Visa **delivery** Free locally, £8.50 per case elsewhere. **G M T**
✪ *Italy, Australia and New Zealand are all marvellous here. France is good and Spain is clearly an enthusiasm, too.*

Vin du Van

mail order Colthups, The Street, Appledore, Kent TN26 2BX (01233) 758727 **fax** (01233) 758389
website www.vinduvan.co.uk **hours** Mon–Fri 9–5 **cards** Delta, Maestro, MasterCard, Visa
delivery Free locally; elsewhere £7.95 for 1st case, further cases free. For Highlands and islands, ask for quote
minimum order 1 mixed case. **M**
✪ *Extensive, wonderfully quirky, star-studded Australian list, one of the best in the UK; the kind of inspired lunacy I'd take to*
read on a desert island.

Vinceremos

mail order Royal House, Sovereign Street, Leeds LS1 4BJ (0800) 107 3086 fax (0113) 288 4566
email info@vinceremos.co.uk website www.vinceremos.co.uk hours Mon–Fri 8.30–5.30
cards AmEx, Delta, Maestro, MasterCard, Visa discounts 5% on 5 cases or more, 10% on 10 cases or more
delivery Free 5 cases or more. M
❂ *Organic specialist, with a wide-ranging list of wines, including biodynamic and Fairtrade. In addition to wine, you can buy fruit wine, beer, cider and perry, spirits and liqueurs.*

Vini Italiani

72 Old Brompton Road, London SW7 3LQ (020) 7225 2283 fax (020) 7225 0848
email info@vini-italiani.co.uk website www.vini-italiani.co.uk hours Mon–Sat 10–10, Sun 11–7
cards AmEx, Delta, Maestro, MasterCard, Visa delivery Free local delivery, cheap London delivery and standard delivery charge for mainland UK minimum order 1 case. C G M T
❂ *Exciting new Italy-only store with fascinating range of classic and non-classic wines. Enomatic sampling machines, courses, masterclasses etc.*

Vintage Roots

mail order Holdshott Farm, Reading Road, Heckfield, Hook, Hampshire RG27 0JZ (0118) 932 6566, (0800) 980 4992
fax (0118) 922 5115 hours Mon–Fri 8.30–5.30, Sat in December email info@vintageroots.co.uk
website www.vintageroots.co.uk cards Delta, Maestro, MasterCard, Visa discounts 5% on 5 cases or over
delivery £6.95 for any delivery under 5 cases; more than 6 cases is free. Some local deliveries free. Cases can be mixed. G M T
❂ *Everything on this list of over 300 wines is certified organic and/or biodynamic. As well as wine, Vintage Roots sell organic beer, cider, liqueurs, spirits and chocolate at Christmas time.*

Virgin Wines

mail order/online The Loft, St James' Mill, Whitefriars, Norwich NR3 1TN 0843 224 1001 fax (01603) 619277
email help@virginwines.co.uk website www.virginwines.co.uk hours (Office) Mon–Fri 8–8, Sat–Sun 9–6
cards AmEx, Maestro, MasterCard, Visa, Paypal delivery £6.99 per order for all UK deliveries
minimum order 1 case. M T
❂ *Online retailer celebrated its first decade in 2010. Reasonably priced wines from all over the world. Additional features include a Wine Bank to help you save for your next case and online auctions.*

Waitrose

head office Doncastle Road, Southern Industrial Area, Bracknell, Berkshire RG12 8YA **customer service** 0800 188884, 228 licensed stores **email** customer_service@waitrose.co.uk **website** www.waitrosewine.com
hours see www.waitrose.com for branch opening hours **cards** AmEx, Delta, Maestro, MasterCard, Partnership Card, Visa
discounts Regular monthly promotions, 5% off for 6 bottles or more
home delivery Available through www.waitrosedeliver.com and www.ocado.com and Waitrose Wine Direct (*below*)
en primeur Bordeaux and Burgundy available through Waitrose Wine Direct. **G M T**
• **waitrose wine direct** order online at www.waitrosewine.com or 0800 188881
email wineadvisor@johnlewis.com **discounts** Vary monthly on featured cases; branch promotions are matched.
All cases include a 5% discount to match branch offer. **delivery** Free standard delivery throughout UK mainland, Northern Ireland and Isle of Wight. Named day delivery, £6.95 per addressee (order by 6pm for next day – not Sun); next-day delivery before 10.30am, £9.95 per addressee (order by 6pm for next working day).
✪ *Ahead of the other supermarkets in quality, value and imagination. Still lots of tasty stuff under £6.*

Waterloo Wine Co

office and warehouse 6 Vine Yard, London SE1 1QL **shop** 59–61 Lant Street, London SE1 1QN (020) 7403 7967
fax (020) 7357 6976 **email** sales@waterloowine.co.uk **website** www.waterloowine.co.uk
hours Mon–Fri 11–7.30, Sat 10–5 **cards** AmEx, Maestro, MasterCard, Visa **delivery** Free 1 case central London; elsewhere, 1 case £12, 2 cases £7.50 each. **G T**
✪ *Quirky, personal list, strong in the Loire and New Zealand.*

Wimbledon Wine Cellar

1 Gladstone Road, Wimbledon, London SW19 1QU (020) 8540 9979 **fax** (020) 8540 9399
email enquiries@wimbledonwinecellar.com **hours** Mon–Sat 10–9
• 84 Chiswick High Road, London W4 1SY (020) 8994 7989 **fax** (020) 8994 3683
email chiswick@wimbledonwinecellar.com **hours** Mon–Sat 10–9
• 4 The Boulevard, Imperial Wharf, Chelsea, London SW6 2UB (020) 7736 2191
email chelsea@wimbledonwinecellar.com **hours** Mon–Sat 10–9, Sun 11–7
website www.wimbledonwinecellar.com **cards** AmEx, Maestro, MasterCard, Visa **discounts** 10% off 1 case (with a few exceptions), 20% off case of 6 Champagne **delivery** Free local delivery. Courier charges elsewhere
en primeur Burgundy, Bordeaux, Tuscany, Rhône. **C G M T**
✪ *Top names from Italy, Burgundy, Bordeaux, Rhône, Loire – and some of the best of the New World.*

Wine & Beer World (Majestic)

head office Majestic House, Otterspool Way, Watford, Hertfordshire WD25 8WW (01923) 298200
email info@wineandbeer.co.uk website www.majesticinfrance.co.uk

• Rue du Judée, Zone Marcel Doret, Calais 62100, France (00 33) 3 21 97 63 00 email calais@majestic.co.uk
hours 7 days 8–8, including Bank Holidays

• Centre Commercial Carrefour, Quai L'Entrepôt, Cherbourg 50100, France (00 33) 2 33 22 23 22
email cherbourg@majestic.co.uk hours Mon–Sat 9–7

• Unit 3A, Zone La Française, Coquelles 62331, France (00 33) 3 21 82 93 64 email coquelles@majestic.co.uk
hours 7 days 9–7, including Bank Holidays

pre-order (01923) 298297 discounts Available for large pre-orders cards Maestro, MasterCard, Visa. T

○ *The French arm of Majestic, with 300 wines at least £2 less per bottle than Majestic UK prices. Calais is the largest
branch and Coquelles the nearest to the Channel Tunnel terminal. English-speaking staff.*

The Wine Company (Devon)

mail order Town Barton, Doddiscombsleigh, Nr Exeter, Devon EX6 7PT (01647) 252005 email nick@thewinecompany.biz
website www.thewinecompany.biz hours Mon–Sun 9–6 cards Maestro, MasterCard, Visa delivery £7.99 per case, free for
orders over £150, UK mainland only. M

○ *The list of around 250 wines specializes in Australia and South Africa, with some top names you won't find anywhere else.*

The Wine Company (Essex)

Gosbecks Park, Colchester, Essex CO2 9JT (01206) 713560 fax (01206) 713515 email sales@thewinecompany.co.uk
website www.thewinecompany.co.uk hours Mon–Sat 9–6 cards Delta, Electron, MasterCard, Maestro, Switch, Visa
delivery £7.99 or free for orders over £200 within UK mainland; please ring or email for quote for Highlands, islands and
Northern Ireland. C G M T

○ *Family-owned wine merchant, strong in French wines and wines from smaller estates, with plenty under £10.
Well-chosen mixed case offers and regular tastings and dinners.*

Wine Pantry

1 Stoney Street, Borough Market, London SE1 9AA (020) 7403 3003 email info@winepantry.co.uk
website www.winepantry.co.uk hours Tues, Wed and Sat 12–8, Thur–Fri 12–10 cards Delta, Electron, MasterCard,
Maestro, Switch, Visa delivery UK mainland; visit the website for other delivery details, including international. M T

○ *Extensive list of quality English still and sparkling wines, plus English cheeses and cured meats.*

Wine Rack

head office Venus House, Brantwood Road, London N17 0YD (020) 8801 0011 **fax** (020) 8801 6455
email info@winerack.co.uk **website** www.winerack.co.uk; 19 Wine Rack stores and more to come
hours Mon–Sat 10–10, Sun 11–10 **cards** Maestro, MasterCard, Visa **delivery** Free locally, some branches. **G T**
✪ *Following the collapse in 2009 of First Quench (aka Thresher's and Wine Rack) a new owner has bought the Wine Rack name and revitalized a selection of Wine Rack stores in London, Bristol and the Home Counties.*

The Wine Society

mail order/online Gunnels Wood Road, Stevenage, Herts SG1 2BG (01438) 741177 **fax** (01438) 761167
order line (01438) 740222 **email** memberservices@thewinesociety.com **website** www.thewinesociety.com
hours Mon–Fri 8.30–9, Sat 9–5; showroom: Mon–Fri 10–6, Thur 10–7, Sat 9.30–5.30
cards Delta, Maestro, MasterCard, Visa **discounts** (per case) £3 for pre-ordered collection **delivery** Free 1 case or more
anywhere in UK; also collection facility at Templepatrick, County Antrim, and showroom and collection facility at Montreuil,
France, at French rates of duty and VAT **en primeur** Bordeaux, Burgundy, Germany, Port, Rhône. **C G M T**
✪ *An outstanding list from an inspired wine-buying team. Masses of well-chosen affordable wines as well as big names. The Wine Society regularly wins the UK's top awards for wine by mail order. Founded in 1874, The Wine Society's aim was, and remains, to introduce members to the best of the world's vineyards at a fair price. Holding a share in The Wine Society gives you a lifetime membership with no annual fee and no pressure to buy. The cost of a share is £40.*

The Wine Treasury

mail order 69–71 Bondway, London SW8 1SQ (020) 7793 9999
fax (020) 7793 8080 **email** bottled@winetreasury.com **website** www.winetreasury.com **hours** Mon–Fri 9.30–6
cards AmEx, Maestro, MasterCard, Visa **discounts** 10% for unmixed dozens **delivery** Free for orders over £300,
England and Wales; Scotland phone for more details **minimum order** 1 mixed case. **M**
✪ *Excellent choices and top names from California and Italy – but they don't come cheap.*

Winemark the Wine Merchants

3 Duncrue Place, Belfast BT3 9BU (028) 9074 6274 **fax** (028) 9074 8022; 77 branches **email** info@winemark.com
website www.winemark.com **hours** Branches vary, but in general Mon–Sat 10–10, Sun 12–8
cards Switch, MasterCard, Visa **discounts** 5% on 6–11 bottles, 10% on 12 bottles or more. **G M T**
✪ *Over 500 wines, with some interesting wines from Australia, New Zealand, Chile and California.*

The Winery

4 Clifton Road, London W9 1SS (020) 7286 6475 fax (020) 7286 2733 email info@thewineryuk.com
website www.thewineryuk.com hours Mon–Sat 11–9.30, Sun and public holidays 12–8
cards Maestro, MasterCard, Visa discounts 5% on a mixed case delivery Free locally or for 3 cases or more,
 otherwise £10 per case. **G M T**
❂ *Largest selection of dry German wines in the UK. Burgundy, Rhône, Champagne, Italy and California are other specialities.*

WoodWinters

16 Henderson Street, Bridge of Allan, Scotland FK9 4HP (01786) 834894
• 91 Newington Road, Edinburgh EH9 1QW (0131) 667 2760
email shop@woodwinters.com website www.woodwinters.com hours Mon–Sat 10–7; Sun 1–5
cards MasterCard, Switch, Visa discounts Vintners Dozen: buy 12 items or more and get a 13th free – we are happy to
choose something appropriate for you delivery £8.95 per address; free for orders over £150 UK mainland. Islands and
Northern Ireland, phone for quote en primeur Bordeaux, Burgundy, Italy, Rhone. **C G M T**
❂ *A young, ambitious operation, very strong on California and Australia, but also good stuff from Austria, Portugal, Italy,*
Spain and Burgundy. They do like flavour, *so expect most of their wines to be mouth-filling. Wine tasting club and courses.*

Wright Wine Co

The Old Smithy, Raikes Road, Skipton, North Yorkshire BD23 1NP (0800) 328 4435 fax (01756) 798580
email enquiries@wineandwhisky.co.uk website www.wineandwhisky.co.uk hours Mon–Fri 9–6; Sat 10–5:30; open
Sundays in December 11–3 cards Maestro, MasterCard, Visa discounts 10% unsplit case, 5% mixed case
delivery Free within 30 miles, elsewhere at cost. **G**
❂ *Equally good in both Old World and New World, with plenty of good stuff at keen prices. Wide choice of half bottles.*

Peter Wylie Fine Wines

Plymtree Manor, Plymtree, Cullompton, Devon EX15 2LE (01884) 277555 fax (01884) 277557
email peter@wyliefinewines.co.uk website www.wyliefinewines.co.uk hours Mon–Fri 9–5.30
discounts Only on unsplit cases delivery Up to 3 cases in London £30, otherwise by arrangement. **C M**
❂ *Fascinating list of mature wines: Bordeaux from throughout the 20th century, vintage ports going back to the 1920s.*

The following services are available where indicated: C = cellarage **G** = glass hire/loan **M** = mail/online order **T** = tastings and talks

Yapp Brothers

shop The Old Brewery, Water Street, Mere, Wiltshire BA12 6DY (01747) 860423 fax (01747) 860929
email sales@yapp.co.uk website www.yapp.co.uk hours Mon–Sat 9–6 cards Maestro, MasterCard, Visa
discounts £6 per case on collection delivery £8 one case, 2 or more cases free. C G M T
❍ *Rhône and Loire specialists. Also some of the hard-to-find wines of Provence, Savoie, South-West France and Corsica, plus a small selection from Australia.*

Noel Young Wines

56 High Street, Trumpington, Cambridge CB2 9LS (01223) 566744 fax (01223) 844736
email admin@nywines.co.uk website www.nywines.co.uk hours Mon–Fri 10–8, Sat 10–7, Sun 12–2
cards AmEx, Maestro, MasterCard, Visa discounts 5% for orders over £500 delivery Free over 12 bottles unless discounted en primeur Australia, Burgundy, Italy, Rhône. G M T
❍ *Fantastic wines from just about everywhere. Australia is a particular passion and there is a great Austrian list, some terrific Germans, plus beautiful Burgundies, Italians and dessert wines.*

Who's where

COUNTRYWIDE/MAIL ORDER/ONLINE
Adnams
Aldi
ASDA
AustralianWineCentre
Bancroft Wines
Bibendum Wine
Big Red Wine Co
Bordeaux Index
Anthony Byrne
Cockburns of Leith
Co-op
Devigne Wines
Nick Dobson Wines
Domaine Direct
FromVineyardsDirect
Roger Harris Wines
Jeroboams
Justerini & Brooks
Laithwaites
Lay & Wheeler
Laytons
Liberty Wines
O W Loeb
Majestic
Marks & Spencer
Millésima
Montrachet
Morrisons
New Zealand House of Wine
OZ WINES
Private Cellar
Real Wine Co
Howard Ripley
Sainsbury's
Stone, Vine & Sun

Sunday Times Wine Club
Swig
Tesco
Vin du Van
Vinceremos
Vintage Roots
Virgin Wines
Waitrose
The Wine Company
The Wine Society
The Wine Treasury
Peter Wylie Fine Wines
Yapp Brothers
Noel Young Wines

LONDON
Armit
Berkmann Wine Cellars
Berry Bros. & Rudd
Budgens
Corney & Barrow
Farr Vintners
Fortnum & Mason
Friarwood
Goedhuis & Co
Green & Blue
Handford Wines
Harvey Nichols
Haynes Hanson & Clark
Jeroboams
Lea & Sandeman
Moreno Wines
Philglas & Swiggot
Roberson
RSJ Wine Company
The Sampler
Selfridges
Waterloo Wine Co

Wimbledon Wine Cellar
Wine Rack
The Winery

SOUTH-EAST AND HOME COUNTIES
A&B Vintners
Berry Bros. & Rudd
Budgens
Butlers Wine Cellar
Les Caves de Pyrene
Flagship Wines
Hedley Wright
Maison du Vin
Quaff
Turville Valley Wines
Wine Rack

WEST AND SOUTH-WEST
Averys Wine Merchants
Bennetts Fine Wines
Berkmann Wine Cellars
Great Western Wine
Haynes Hanson & Clark
Hicks & Don
Old Chapel Cellars
Christopher Piper Wines
Reid Wines
Savage Selection
Wine Rack
Peter Wylie Fine Wines
Yapp Brothers

EAST ANGLIA
Adnams
Budgens
Anthony Byrne

Cambridge Wine Merchants
Corney & Barrow
Seckford Wines
T & W Wines
Noel Young Wines

MIDLANDS
Bat & Bottle
Connolly's
Gauntleys
Harvey Nichols
S H Jones
Nickolls & Perks
Noble Rot Wine Warehouses
Oxford Wine Co
Selfridges
Stevens Garnier
Tanners

NORTH
Berkmann Wine Cellars
Booths
D Byrne
deFINE Food and Wine
Great Northern Wine
Halifax Wine Co
hangingditch
Harvey Nichols
Martinez Wines
Nidderdale Fine Wines
Penistone Court
Portland Wine Co
Reserve Wines
Selfridges
Stainton Wines
Terroir Languedoc

House of Townend
Wright Wine Co

WALES
Fingal-Rock
Terry Platt
Tanners

SCOTLAND
Corney & Barrow
Friarwood
Peter Green & Co
Harvey Nichols
Linlithgow Wines
Raeburn Fine Wines
Valvona & Crolla
Villeneuve Wines
WoodWinters

IRELAND
Direct Wine Shipments
James Nicholson
O'Briens
Winemark

CHANNEL ISLANDS
Sommelier Wine Co

FRANCE
Millésima
Wine & Beer World
The Wine Society